THE FICTIONAL

CHILDREN OF

HENRY JAMES

THE FICTIONAL
CHILDREN OF
Henry James

BY MURIEL G. SHINE

THE UNIVERSITY OF
NORTH CAROLINA PRESS
CHAPEL HILL

FOR *Ezra* AND *Daniel*

Preface

There is good reason for isolating children and the themes of childhood and adolescence in the novels and tales of Henry James. Not only did he devote the better part of a decade to writing about young people in a strikingly modern way, but his early critical reviews, his travel sketches, and his autobiography abound in observations on children, child-rearing, and the maturing process. Indeed, implicit in these novels and tales one could say there is a significant "theory of education."

James's first published tale, "A Tragedy of Error," has a child in it. At least nine other tales written between 1864 and 1891 make reference to or involve children. Adolescence and the maturing process are thematically important in his first novel, *Watch and Ward*. Children figure prominently in *Daisy Miller* and *The Portrait of a Lady*. Between 1891 and 1899 three important tales—"The Pupil," "The Turn of the Screw," "In the Cage"—and two novels—*What Maisie Knew* and *The Awkward Age*—have as focal characters young people who take command of the scene; their perception of evil and their effort to triumph over a corrupt environment constitutes the dramatic action. In the 1890's James gave us such memorable child-characters as Morgan Moreen, Maisie Farange, Flora and Miles, and that first in a long line of twentieth-century troubled and "aware" adolescents, Nanda Brookenham. Such preoccupation with the themes of childhood and growth on the part of an author as perceptive and "psychological" as Henry James is significant; it suggests that a careful study of his fictional representation of children, childhood, and adolescence might yield a total view of his attitudes toward family relations and a sense of how the young should be reared.

While James's fictional children and their relevance to his art have been discussed from time to time by critics and scholars, no detailed study of them has been made. I have made no attempt to discuss the stories in any context other than that of the novelist's treatment of children and the vision of childhood and adolescence which that treatment reflects. While I have noted social and historical factors that may have affected James's rendering of children and adolescents, the major emphasis is on the identification, analysis, and synthesis of diverse thematic patterns which fused in the 1890's to produce the uniquely Jamesian child.

I wish to express my appreciation and gratitude to Professor Leon Edel for encouraging me to undertake this study and for his infinite patience in offering much-needed guidance and criticism in all phases of this project. I am grateful as well to the Faculty Committee on Scholarly Research at Pace College, New York, for the special grant that helped subsidize this publication.

Acknowledgments

I would like to thank the following authors and publishers whose copyrighted works have been quoted in the text:

Cambridge University Press: *Children's Books in England* by F. J. Harvey Darton; *The Ordeal of Consciousness* by Dorothea Krook.

Charles Scribner's Sons: *The Art of the Novel* by Henry James, edited by R. P. Blackmur; *What Maisie Knew* by Henry James.

E. P. Dutton & Co., Inc.: *Selected Fiction of Henry James* edited by Leon Edel.

Harper and Row: *The Awkward Age* by Henry James.

The Horn Book, Inc.: *Les Livres, Les Enfants et Les Hommes* by Paul Hazard.

The Macmillan Company: *The Princess Casamassima* by Henry James.

Random House, Inc.: *The Portrait of a Lady* by Henry James; *The Bostonians* by Henry James.

A Note on Texts Used

In comparing the original magazine texts of the tales with those published in book form soon afterwards, no significant revisions pertinent to my topic were found. All references to the tales will therefore be from *The Complete Tales of Henry James,* 12 vols., ed. Leon Edel. New York and London, 1961–64. These volumes make use of the first book publication of the tales. All references to the novels are based on the New York Edition of *The Novels and Tales of Henry James,* 1907–9 (reprinted 1961–65) except where quotations from earlier texts may be relevant to my discussion or where references are made to novels not included in the New York Edition. For a complete list of the writings of Henry James see *A Bibliography of Henry James* by Leon Edel and Dan H. Laurence, London, 1957; second revised edition, 1961.

Contents

THE FICTIONAL
CHILDREN OF
HENRY JAMES

Children in Literature
Introduction

It may be difficult for the reader of twentieth-century
fiction to think of a time when the theme of childhood
had no place in literature. While children figured from
time to time in poetry and drama from Homer through
Shakespeare, they were not considered thematically important, nor were they rendered as individual personalities. Until the end of the neoclassical era, childhood was
a period rapidly passed over. The cognitive faculty in its
most highly developed form, the adult passions, engaged
the imagination of the artist. Rational man in conflict
with an impersonal universe was the theme of preroman-
tic literature; the unformed, unthinking child had no role
to play in it. The Greeks, with their emphasis on the su-
premacy of the mind in the affairs of men, found little
more in the child than a symbol of perpetuity or an echo
of adult sentiment. Astynaax, Hector's "sweet child" in
Euripides' *Trojan Women*, is witness to the disasters of
war; he gives no evidence, however, of having been affected by the tragedy that has befallen Troy. He is torn
from his mother's side without having uttered a sound.
When Medea's children speak, it is to express adult fear
and terror in the face of disorder and violence.

The Elizabethan, Jacobean, and Restoration dramatists
and poets, like their predecessors, did not consider the
child a suitable medium through which to comment on
the condition of man. To be sure, the child had always
been a symbol of innocence and an object of compassion
—this is deeply rooted in the Christian tradition—but
earlier than the last decades of the eighteenth century,

neither the symbol nor the feeling appeared in literature.

The child first appears prominently in romantic poetry at the end of the eighteenth century as the poet began to attend to feeling as well as mind. The artist's reaction against social disorder and spiritual aridity brought a recognition of the child as a felicitous image of lost innocence. Traditionally the child elicited feelings of tenderness and pathos and had always been considered in need of adult guidance and protection; how logical, then, for the helplessness of childhood to become emblematic of man's precarious position in a rapidly changing world. Poets like William Blake and William Wordsworth, in a time of political revolution and industrialization, seized upon the child as a symbol of simplicity and spirituality in an increasingly complex materialistic world. Childhood became a metaphor for the ideal human condition. "The child," Peter Coveney remarks, "could serve as a symbol of the artist's dissatisfaction with society which was in process of such harsh development about him." [1] More, the artist could create the child in his own image; he could voice his anxieties, project his fears through the theme of childhood. The "cry of the children" became the cry of the creative artist seeking security in an unstable world.

In the untainted quality of childhood and the inevitable loss of youthful innocence, William Blake found the metaphor to dramatize his theme of the coexistence of good and evil in man. Blake's was neither a naïve nor optimistic view of childhood. He recognized the reality of evil in the child's as well as the adult's world, and his multilateral view of life prevented him from accepting childhood as a time of unalloyed joy. The poet, however, had a deeply felt need for joyous affirmation of life and this he expressed through imagining childhood as a time of innocence and peace. The condition of innocence might be precarious in Blake's world, but it could, nevertheless, stand as a moment of surcease in man's continuing internal conflict. Good and evil are comingled in Blake's

---

1. Peter Coveney, *Poor Monkey: The Child in Literature* (London, 1957), Introduction, p. xi.

world, and his vision of the child as the embodiment of innocence made recognition and acceptance of evil bearable. It is evident that through the image of the child, Blake, the Christian mystic, could effect total identification with his God:

> Sweet babe, in thy face
> Holy image I can trace
> Sweet babe, once like thee
> Thy Maker lay and wept for me.

Blake could create a serenity unobtainable in the real world by projecting the child's world:

> When the voices of children are heard
> on the green
> And laughing is heard on the hill,
> My heart is at rest within my breast,
> And everything else is still.

In many of *The Songs of Innocence* children are pictured with a new concreteness. The child emerges as more than emblematic of an ideal moment in the spiritual development of man. The little chimney sweep is unique in that he is closely observed, realistically presented, and endowed with an individual point of view. We recognize in him a particular child reacting to a particular environment in a particular way; he is this as well as a symbol of innocence in the midst of social evil. In Blake's poetry, environment impinges directly on the consciousness of the small child, and the wickedness of the adult world is rendered through the sensibilities of the young.

The theme of childhood is so much a part of William Wordsworth's philosophy that it cannot be separated from his vision of life. For Wordsworth childhood was a time of pure sensation, and in this state of sensuous being he held man to be closest to truth and to God. In his scheme of the mental development of man, this is a period of pure pleasure and accordingly the most difficult to relinquish. "The Prelude," and with even more intensity "Ode on Intimations of Immortality," project a reluctance on the part of the poet to move on to the next stage of development; he finds in the unrestrained sensuousness of childhood a vitality and satisfaction that, in spite of his protestation to the contrary, he was not able to derive from the "philosophic mind" that presumably comes with maturity. It is noteworthy that loss of innocence and death are frequently associated in Wordsworth's poetry. Michael's son goes off to the city (Wordsworth's correlative for loss of innocence) and dies there. The boy in "There Was a Boy" was "taken from his mates and died in childhood, ere he was full twelve years old." In the "Lucy" poems (where the mysterious Lucy is sometimes a child and sometimes an adult but always emblematic of lost youth) this apposition of loss of innocence and death is marked. It is as though the end of childhood, and the sensual joy that characterizes it, were a kind of extinction for the poet:

> Three years she grew in sun and shower
> Then Nature said, "A lovelier flower
> On earth was never sown;
> This child I to myself will take;
> She shall be mine, and I will make
> A Lady of my own.

And again:

> She lived unknown, and few could know
>   When Lucy ceased to be
> But she is in her grave, and oh
>   The difference to me!

Blake and Wordsworth helped to create a legend of childhood which embodied the traditional Christian ideal of innocence and purity and which also focused attention on the child as an individual reacting to his environment. This romantic view of the child in late eighteenth- and early nineteenth-century poetry profoundly affected the presentation of children in the literature that followed, particularly in the novel, which became the dominant genre of the nineteenth and twentieth centuries.

Other influences helped determine what forms the theme of childhood in literature would take. Not the least of these was American transcendentalism, with its idealistic view of man and nature and, perhaps more important, its firm belief that virtue and happiness depend upon the fullest self-realization of the individual. The romantic and the transcendental philosophers were, in fact, at one in their glorification of nature and childhood. Thoreau reflects the reverence of his age for youth when he says that "children, who play life, discern its true law and relations more clearly than men, who fail to live it worthily." Like Wordsworth, Thoreau felt that "every child begins the world again." The transcendentalists, with their emphasis on self-reliance and their adherence to the democratic principle, added a new dimension to the portrait of the child. In a land of infinite possibilities, the child was free to develop and even, in some measure, to control his own destiny; it was only necessary that the proper conditions for self-expression prevail. Alfred Kazin observes that "as soon as the beneficent rays of transcendentalism (not to say the growing comfort and secular happiness of middle-class families in virtuous and self-respecting New England, to itself the best of all possible worlds) made the lovable American child as fundamental a type as the self-respecting Yankee, the child in American literature becomes the dear little fellow, the lovable urchin, the professional bad boy—Our Gang." [2]

There is, however, another and more important American fictional child whom I shall discuss in due course; yet one cannot ignore "the lovable urchin" in the evolution of the child in literature. More significant, to my mind, is the fact that the child in American fiction became identified with the youth and potential of the vast, unexplored continent. Some American authors saw in the child not only the essential goodness that is central to an idealistic view of man; they saw as well, a symbol of virgin territory where democracy prevailed and where there were unlimited possibilities for growth.

Other writers took a less benevolent attitude. They saw in the image of the child an opportunity to give free rein

2. Alfred Kazin, "A Procession of Children," *The American Scholar* (Spring, 1964), p. 173.

to the Puritan bent toward inner scrutiny, the psychological strain that we have come to associate with the best examples of American fictional children. These novelists had a most profound and lasting effect on the development of the fictional child. Nathaniel Hawthorne and Mark Twain, in their preoccupation with the nature of evil and the extent of man's moral responsibility, used the child to express their uncertainty and to dramatize the quest for answers to complex and often unanswerable questions about the nature of man's destiny. They discovered depths of perception in the child and explored, through its consciousness, aspects of the human dilemma that had heretofore been the exclusive province of adult characters in fiction.

The Puritans, with their commitment to the doctrine of original sin, had traditionally conceived of the child as wicked. Hawthorne explored in his tales the "instinct of destruction" and "the terrible precocity" of children and, in so doing, helped to create a more complex fictional child. F. O. Matthiessen, in *The American Renaissance*, called Hawthorne one of the "nay sayers," one of those writers who was out of step with the optimistic trend of his time. Because he was unable to take a positive view of human nature, his children have a capacity for evil and a tendency toward introspection missing in the conventional image of the "pure" child in fiction. With his allegorical method and his use of limited symbols, Hawthorne created a unique child, half real, half imaginary, one who thereby expressed his tragic vision of life.

The advance of the nineteenth century brought ever more burdensome social and psychological problems, a result of urbanization, and, most unsettling of all, the failure of traditional beliefs. The creed of progress, with concomitant materialism, the doctrines of evolution and determinism, with their death-dealing blow to an ancient faith, created an atmosphere of tension that artists felt and reflected. Writers of the period sought to come to terms with inconsistencies among prevailing philosophic, scientific, and economic doctrines. Some novelists, on both sides of the Atlantic, touched by the child-victims of industrialization and drawing on their feelings or childhood experiences, directly criticized those aspects of society which were abhorrent to them. Charles Dickens, early in the century, transformed the "innocent" and "pure" child of romantic poetry into the brutalized and exploited child-victim of aggressive, unfeeling adults. An ardent advocate of reform, the novelist made the child voice his protest against dehumanizing forces in society.

Oliver Twist contains the first harbinger of what was to become a recurring theme in Dickens. Oliver is the prototype of the passive, disinherited child who was to dominate the author's novels of social protest. The boy-hero is presented as a powerless pawn of forces beyond his control; he is buffeted by the agents of good and evil alike, taking no active part in the struggle for his own salvation. Steven Marcus notes: "He is active in a way that a ball batted back and forth between opposing sides is active. Oliver is essentially the incarnation of a moral quality, and the particular virtue he represents requires that he appear all but defenseless. For he is ideal and incorruptible innocence." [3]

While *Oliver Twist* is a satire on the Poor Law of 1834, its hero radiates an innocence and a lack of involvement with the central issue unusual for the genre. This is because Dickens' children are first and foremost exploited victims; who or what his boy-hero is exploited *by* is actually of secondary importance. The fact of the child's brutalization is of primary concern to Dickens. The novelist empathized with children to an unusual degree, a capacity that had its origin in his own difficult childhood. He was never able to free himself from the sense of humiliation and abandonment he felt at his father's incarceration in Marshalsea Prison for debts and his own enforced labor at twelve in Warren's blacking warehouse.

Dickens' treatment of children became more complex as he matured and mastered his art. His children developed a consciousness of self, and with this consciousness came the need for self-discovery, self-identification, and

3. Steven Marcus, *Dickens: From Pickwick to Dombey* (New York, 1965), p. 80.

self-realization. The beginning of the quest for identity is seen in *David Copperfield;* in *Great Expectations* Dickens treats his theme more fully and with greater profundity. Pip, with his unrealistic sense of guilt because he was "raised by the hand" in his sister's home and his need, as a result, to expiate his "crime" by being something other than he is, is a penetrating study of the impact of the emotional environment on the personality of the child. With Pip's discovery of self comes an awareness of the moral obligation to those around him, a necessary condition for coming to terms with one's self and the society in which one lives. Dickens made the consciousness of the child a field of investigation for the novelist; more, he proved that the sensibility of the young can be an effective gauge of adult values.

Nearly two decades after Dickens, Mark Twain unmasked the hypocrisy and ambiguity of society in nineteenth-century America through the consciousness of a boy. In *Huckleberry Finn* the novelist produced what is perhaps the finest story in the English language of youth's search for values in a warped society. In this work Twain fused the traditional materials of humor, folkways, legend, and boyhood experience to create a memorable critique of man's inhumanity. Huck observes the world with a disillusioned eye. He does constant battle with hypocritical, violent, and cruel adults. He sees life for what it is, but he sees it through the eyes of a boy; his voice is a boy's voice, and he seems to stand apart from his experience. For a larger part of the novel he is the uncommitted observer, disengaged in spite of his involvement with the characters and events of the story. We discern in Twain the beginning of the idea that children are a species apart. This notion of the child as having an autonomous existence is characteristic of the twentieth-century attitude.

While Huck is a creature apart, uninvolved, he possesses an inner morality that, at the crucial moment, impels him to act decisively. This is presented as inherent in the boy. Huck did not acquire it through instruction, nor did he absorb it from the behavior of the adults around him. Huck is closer to God and truth in the Wordsworthian sense—by virtue of the fact that he is a child. He is presented as having what William Walsh calls "a genuine unforced moral impulse, the moral correlation of the free flowing life of the river." [4] This view of Huck as intrinsically good is romantic. It does not give due emphasis to the fact that the boy's inner struggle comprises the essential dramatic action of the novel. The voyage down the river chronicles Huck's spiritual growth. Through his increasing awareness of what constitutes truly moral behavior he comes to accept love and loyalty as the only possible criteria for distinguishing between right and wrong. "All right then," says Huck, when he decides not to turn Jim in, "I'll *go* to hell!" The moral sense has ultimately triumphed over the "civilization" with which it has been in conflict.

Innocence is no prerequisite for moral excellence in Twain's world; indeed, only through perception, awareness, the acquisition of a maturity that requires *loss* of innocence, can one hope to become truly virtuous. Huck suggests more than innocence lost and virtue gained, however. Like the river, the central symbol of the novel, Huck dramatizes a continental myth. Mark Twain felt that something valuable in American life had been lost after the Civil War, something this vast young continent could ill afford to relinquish, some value, some faith in the essential goodness of man. Huck's voyage is a quest for the regeneration of a continent. In Mark Twain's portrait of the child, one observes the fusion of three distinct traditions in the treatment of children in literature: the Wordsworthian child as symbol of purity and inherent goodness; the American child as emblematic of the possibilities inherent in a vast and virgin land; and the Puritan child as the embodiment of the analytic, introspective mind concerned with the nature of good and evil. The comingling of these diverse views of the child is Mark Twain's major contribution to the evolution of the child in literature.

For other American and English novelists, the litera-

4. William Walsh, *The Uses of the Imagination* (New York, 1960), p. 148.

ture of nostalgia or tales of adventure offered a solution to the vexing problems of the age. The romantic concept of the child persisted in its appeal to writer and reader alike. The serenity and peace of an idealized, long-ago-and-far-away childhood, the retrospective glamour of school days, or the excitement of improbable adventures on non-existent islands offered refuge from the turmoil of an industrial age. John Jay Bell, Samuel Rutherford Crockett, and, most widely acclaimed of the Kailyard school of literature, J. M. Barrie, Rudyard Kipling, and Robert Louis Stevenson, all gratified their own as well as a broad reading public's need for flight from reality. Social conditions in the last decades of the nineteenth century made this kind of literature immensely popular in Great Britain and the United States. Bell's *Wee Macgreegor,* a tale of a vivacious, inquisitive youngster of sturdy artisan stock, was but one example of the effort on the part of author and reader to turn from harsh reality through adherence to "the cult of the child." The Kailyard or "cabbage-patch" school of literature, characterized by its focus on themes of domesticity and rustic humor, was essentially Scottish in origin and testifies to the strength and breadth of the impulse to seek retreat in homely tales of carefree childhood. Paul Hazard, in his discussion of the character of children's books in France, England, Germany, and Italy from the seventeenth to the twentieth century observes that a sentimental view of childhood seems to be rooted in the Nordic personality.[5] Much of the literature of this period seems to support his contention that Nordic people retain the sense of childhood longer than others and that they look upon adults as grown-up children. American and British writers glorified childhood and a broad reading public shared this sentiment. Fiction of this kind tended to erase the distinction between child and adult; the juvenile and mature reading public overlapped and sentimentality was the order of the day.

J. M. Barrie's *Peter Pan* was the outstanding example of the triumph of sentimentality over British and American

5. Paul Hazard, *Les Livres, Les Enfants et Les Hommes* (Paris, 1932), pp. 172–73.

taste during the latter part of the nineteenth century. This tale, and its subsequent dramatization, created a new school; hundreds of fictional children were to bring tears of joy to the eyes of a public yearning to relive the relatively harmless adventures of childhood, to experience once more childish fears that had no basis in reality.

The quality of these books varied from author to author. Some writers were able to capture the mythic aspect of the adventure of childhood and universalize their theme. These works have become classic examples of the genre. The adventure stories of Robert Louis Stevenson embody some of the best characteristics of this literature. Henry James, friend and admirer of Stevenson, wrote that this author gave "to the world the romance of boyhood, as others have produced that of the peerage and the police and the medical profession." In an illuminating discussion of children's books in England, F. J. Harvey Darton suggests the source of Stevenson's appeal: "He had always been a boy at heart. . . . He knew now that other grown men wanted to remain young . . . that was the real secret: not that boys delighted in tales meant for men, like *Robinson Crusoe* . . . but that men—Victorian men—were eager for tales meant for boys, like *Treasure Island*." [6]

Darton traces the evolution of the title of the popular magazine in which *Treasure Island* was serialized in 1881. His purpose is to demonstrate that the sequence of alterations in the title of this journal reflects the change that was taking place in the reading habits of the public:

July, 1876.	*Young Folks' Weekly Budget.*
July, 1879.	*Young Folks.*
December, 1884.	*Young Folks' Paper.*
July, 1891.	*Old and Young.*
September, 1896.	*Folks at Home.*

Darton further suggests:

Stevenson and [Rider] Haggard both realized, consciously or unconsciously, the need of something more than adventure undertaken in an atmosphere of "manliness." The events must

6. F. J. Harvey Darton, *Children's Books in England* (Cambridge, Eng., 1932), p. 301–2.

be swift and stirring, but that is not enough . . . [characters] must have marked idiosyncracies. But equally they must not be grotesques, suddenly triumphant or cast down. . . . They must in short be probable improbabilities—a necessity of romance as well as of Aristotelian tragedy.

That was an entirely new note in fiction for the young, just as was the deliberate fusion of father and son into one reader.[7]

Although the "romance of boyhood" was, in the twentieth century, to evolve into the "problem of boyhood," the proliferation of contemporary novels about childhood written for mature consumption suggests that Stevenson and other novelists of his time with similar subjects made the theme of adventurous childhood and the enterprising child-hero significant for adult readers.

Thomas Hughes's widely read *Tom Brown's School Days* paved the way for later novels in which life at the English public school was fictionalized. Here was another experience of childhood which appealed to reader and writer alike. The carefree and irresponsible period of school life evoked readers' memories of their own school-days; it was a return to boyhood and was beguiling to those overburdened with individual and social responsibilities. If the schoolboy was not totally unrestrained, at least his accountability was minimal; he needed only to conform to a simple and comprehensible code of behavior.

Rudyard Kipling's *Stalky & Co.* was one of many novels that permitted the reader to relive, in fantasy, his carefree schooldays. Kipling was most successful when he dealt specifically with youthful irresponsibility, less so when he invoked schoolboy morality. This morality, however, appealed to the unsophisticated reader. The novelist's school-boys enabled the adult reader to experience, albeit vicariously, brutality and violence presented within a socially acceptable code of behavior. The school bully always got his just deserts, but, before right triumphed over might, the reader was able to release much pent up hostility. If we accept the notion that our attitude toward children is, in part, a reflection of how we feel about ourselves, then Kipling's image of the child gives us a glimpse of the baser

7. Ibid., pp. 303–4.

and more primitive side of man. The fact that the author presented this aspect of human nature in socially sanctioned terms probably accounts for the popularity of this kind of fiction. The reader can, as it were, have his cake and eat it too; he can have fantasies of violence; he can identify with the brute, and, in the end, it is alright because "boys will be boys" and, after all, they do adhere to the rules of the game. Kipling's exposition of the violence and brutality of childhood was to benefit twentieth-century child portraitists. Unlike Kipling, who exalted these qualities, later writers were to deplore them and seek to uncover the roots of destructive impulses.

Yet another fictional child gained prominence in the novels of the time—the sentimental, maudlin child. The boy-hero of Frances Hodgson Burnett's *Little Lord Fauntleroy* is an outstanding example of the type. Few stories have enjoyed the popularity of this fable of rags to riches achieved through admirable behavior. The rosy, golden-haired cherub in the velvet suit, son of an English earl and and American commoner, who bridges the social and economic gap by virtue of his sterling character, delighted middle-class readers in both countries. Mr. Gladstone went so far as to remark that the book would help cement the understanding between Britain and the United States. The English prime minister may have exaggerated young Cedric Errol's effect on international relations but there is little doubt that the manly, upright, and fearless little boy, with his blond curls and angelic ways, was to serve as the archetypal saint-child in British and American fiction.

So popular was the image of the pure and noble little man (or woman) that even the sophisticated *Yellow Book* bowed to the temper of the public. This influential journal professed to "treat, not of the passing moment and its interests, but . . . with the permanent and the stable." Yet there appeared in its last issue (April, 1897) a tale that for sheer mawkishness would be difficult to duplicate. "Kit: An American Boy," by Jennie A. Eustace, deals with the loving relationship between a young boy and his mother. It has all the accouterments of the genre, the dying mother, the little hero who saves her life, the trusty steed that gets him to the doctor in time, all this and much more. In the light of Freudian theory, much could be made of a passage like, "He [Kit] knew a dozen little secrets of her [his mother's] toilet, and took pleasure in seeing that she always performed them to the enhancement of her beauty." The author could never anticipate that her touching picture of filial devotion would lend itself so readily to Freudian interpretation; her sole aim, like that of her more talented predecessor, Louisa M. Alcott, was to pluck the heartstrings of a public that wanted desperately to find in childhood a purity of feeling and a capacity for love somehow unobtainable in the adult world.

Mention must be made of a category of writing which greatly influenced subsequent representation of children in fiction. I refer to "nonsense literature" exemplified in England by Edward Lear and Lewis Carroll (Charles Dodgson). This type of fiction has had tremendous vogue in England and America, for it is adult wit disguised as childhood fantasy. In this genre the child is used as instrument of irony and satire. His humorous and fanciful vision of incongruous adult behavior serves to neutralize feelings of anxiety engendered in the real and often irrational world of men. Critics have assumed that nonsense literature reflects the effort of the artist to create a world into which writer and reader can—by observing a set of rules and forms—escape from the humdrum of existence. It has been noted that this kind of fiction suggests the despair of the creative artist at the inconsistencies in his society and reflects "some of the deeper responses of human consciousness." It is generally acknowledged that *Alice in Wonderland*, the nonsense fantasy par excellence, is much more than a nostalgic paean to "childhood and the happy summer days."

In his discussion of *Alice*, William Empson sheds light on the function of the child and the theme of childhood in nonsense fiction: "In this sort of child-cult the child, through a means of imaginative escape, becomes the critic; Alice is the most reasonable and responsible person in the book. This is meant as charmingly pathetic about her as well as satire about her elders, and there is some implication that the sane man can take no other view of the world, even for controlling it, than the child does." [8] Empson suggests that there are many reasons why adults want to be like children again; it may be in order to re-capture the ability to feel vividly or in order to retreat to a period when sexual drives are less troublesome because unrecognizable; perhaps adults wish to be mothered and evade responsibility.

Whether we think of *Alice* as a vehicle for ideas of which Carroll's circle disapproved or whether we see in it "the vital solution to a profound contradiction between acceptance of faith and the excess of reason" as Harry Levin does, the fact remains that the British and Ameri-can public took Alice to its heart. In a world beset by psychological problems created by polarities between sci-ence and religion, the growth of man's technological fa-cility, and the death of his spirit, Alice satisfied a human need for wisdom without loss of innocence and responsi-bility without loss of spontaneity. But Alice's sojourn in Wonderland does more than comment on a topsy-turvy world; it suggests that growing up can be a frightening experience, that childhood is in actuality not the period of pure joy that the Wordsworthian tradition assumes. The world of the child may often be threatening and hos-tile when he has no signposts to guide him. In *Alice in Wonderland* Carroll has, through the consciousness of his central character, conjured up a world that may be closer to the anguish of childhood than to its pleasure. It seems to me that is why Alice lives on. The reader senses that be-hind the half-solemn games and the whimsical recitation of nursery rhymes the struggle to achieve maturity in a bewildering universe is going on. The true significance of Alice's journey through the looking glass is communicated to the reader with unmistakable clarity. Adults know that in childhood a thin line separates the daemons from the angels and, much as we would like it to be otherwise, childhood can easily be a time when daemons lurk behind

8. William Empson, "Alice in Wonderland: The Child as Swain," in *The Critical Performance*, ed. Stanley Edgar Hyman (New York, 1956), p. 136.

every bush. The fanciful child of nonsense fiction helped novelists cross that line in their probing of the consciousness of the young. In many of the fictional portraits of children that were to follow, the daemonic was to prevail.

There is a long and interesting literary road leading from Wordsworth's "simple child, that lightly draws its breath, And feels its life in every limb" to William Golding's Ralph who "wept for the end of innocence, the darkness of Man's heart." And as we look back along that road, we are not surprised to find that the evolution of the child in English and American fiction closely parallels the development of the novel itself from 1830 to 1900. An outstanding characteristic differentiating the modern novel from that of the nineteenth century is the shift in emphasis from concern with external phenomena to preoccupation with inner experience. Novelists became less concerned with plot and action and more concerned with motivation, less with the reality of *things* and more with the reality of emotions. The effort to dramatize the source of human action, to capture and render what Leon Edel calls "the inwardness of experience," distinguishes the twentieth-century novelist. Talented writers of fiction in the nineteenth century increasingly sought to present human consciousness in all its intricacy and with full cognizance of the ambiguous nature of human experience.

With greater psychological depth in the novel came a deepened sense of moral purpose that was to add a new dimension to the perception of the child in literature. Dickens, George Eliot, Henry James, and Joseph Conrad explored the possibilities of human behavior within a given moral frame of reference with an intensity of purpose that was unique in fiction. The inward scrutiny and deepened moral purpose that characterize the development of the novel define, as well, the evolution of the child in literature. The simplistic view of the child yielded to the probing analytic impulse of the writer and the child became a vessel of consciousness to be explored in depth.

The intellectual climate of the last decades of the past century contributed to this fresh concept of the child and childhood. At this time psychology emerged as a scientific discipline. The findings of Darwin, Preyer, Hall, William James, Charcot, and Freud aroused interest in the formative years. As early as 1877, Charles Darwin published what is considered the first objective, detailed study of a child's behavior. "It has long been known," said George Preyer, the German psychologist, "that the development of this regulator [the brain] depends directly upon the impressions received in youth, and thus upon education." [9]

James Sully, the British psychologist, wrote in the same year: "To treat the child's mind as merely a harbourer of fancies, as completely subject to the illusive spell of its bright imagery, would be the grossest injustice . . . the really intelligent children, boys as well as girls, [are] dispassionate and shrewd inquirers into the make of the actual world while ardently engaged in fashioning a brighter one." [10]

G. Stanley Hall, the American psychologist, had this to say:

The adult finds it hard to recall the emotional and instinctive life of the teens which is banished without trace . . . the best observers see but very little of what goes on in the youthful soul, the development of which is largely subterranean . . . few writers have given true pictures of the chief traits of this developmental period. . . .

It is, I believe, high time that ephebic literature should be recognized as a class by itself, and have a place of its own in the history of letters and in criticism. [11]

There was a growing awareness of the importance of early experiences as determinants of adult behavior and habit of mind. Where the romantics had recognized the sentience of childhood, the psychological novelists at the end of the century began systematically to explore it in their fiction. The ideal of youth as a time that *should* be happy remained, but the reality that childhood is a time of isolation and sadness increasingly impinged upon the consciousness of the writer and was reflected in his depic-

9. George W. Preyer, *Mental Development in the Child* (New York, 1895), p. 250.
10. James Sully, *Studies of Childhood* (New York, 1895), p. 64.
11. G. Stanley Hall, *Adolescence* (New York, 1922), I, p. 536 and p. 589, originally published in 1904.

tion of childhood. The vision of childhood as a time of struggle for survival in an hostile adult world, the recognition of the child as an alien, an outsider, had its inception in the nineteenth century and has persisted into our own with the child in literature becoming an increasingly complex reflector of man's inhumanity to man. Fables of childhood envisioned by some novelists of the nineteenth century were rediscovered, refashioned, and more fully explored in the early decades of the twentieth.

In 1929, Richard Hughes set out to explore a theme in *A High Wind in Jamaica,* which had engaged the imagination of Henry James thirty years earlier—the possibility of children as vessels of evil. Like James in "The Turn of the Screw," Hughes is concerned with the corrupting influence of the adult world on the sensibilities of the young.[12] Rather interestingly, the novel is a complete reversal of Barrie's *Peter Pan* and, as such, effectively demonstrates an important shift in attitude toward children and childhood in fiction between 1890 and 1930.

Both *Peter* and *High Wind* deal with children and pirates; in both instances the struggle between the two groups is emblematic of the conflict between good and evil. However, Jonson and Otto, the pirates in *High Wind,* are a far cry from Captain Hook and his "wicked" crew, and Emily, the child, inhabits a sinister world never envisioned by Peter. The pirates of *High Wind* aimlessly kidnap the children, expose them to irrational violence, and finally, for no apparent reason, yield to their kindlier impulses and release their young prisoners only to be betrayed by them. Jonson and Otto are brought to the gallows for a murder committed by Emily; more than this, the men are convicted solely on the testimony of the child. It is an oddly chilling little tale of corruption in which the children emerge as both victimizers and victims of an unconscionable adult world. In *A High Wind in Jamaica,* it is clear that children in fiction have indeed "been made the emotional scapegoats of the modern conscience." [13]

If Richard Hughes projected the child's world as de-

12. Richard Hughes, *A High Wind in Jamaica* (New York, 1929).
13. Ibid., Introduction, xii.

filed, Henry Roth, in *Call It Sleep* (1934) captured a child's vision of his world as nightmare.[14] Young David Schearl is the novel's center of consciousness in the tradition of his nineteenth-century predecessor, Maisie Farange, of *What Maisie Knew*. It is through his eyes that we witness the pain of his isolation and the terror of his experience of childhood. In the boy's sentient response to the world of sights, sounds, and smells there is much that is reminiscent of James's child-heroine. Like Maisie, David lends "to poorer persons and things . . . a precious element of dignity. . . . They become as [he] deals with them, the stuff of poetry and tragedy and art." [15]

He might as well call it sleep. It was only toward sleep that ears had power to cull again and reassemble the shrill cry, the hoarse voice, the scream of fear, the bells, the thick-breathing, the roar of crowds and all sounds that lay fermenting in the vats of silence and the past . . . and feel them all and feel, not pain, not terror, but strangest triumph, strangest acquiescence. One might as well call it sleep. He shut his eyes.[16]

The protest obliquely expressed through the children in *A High Wind in Jamaica* and *Call It Sleep* is explicitly rendered through the tortured consciousness of Holden Caulfield in *The Catcher in the Rye* (1945). Holden, too, has his roots in the nineteenth century. He is strongly suggestive of Daisy Miller's tragicomic young brother, Randolph, grown to adolescence and transported to twentieth-century New York. One suspects that little Randolph C. Miller, dragged unwillingly through Europe and with no sense of belonging anywhere, could conceivably grow into a "catcher in the rye," intent upon preventing children from becoming part of the cold, indifferent, ethically questionable adult world.

Mindful not only of the intellectual climate that nourished Henry James but also of the effect his vision of childhood may have had upon subsequent writers, we may

14. Henry Roth, *Call It Sleep* (New York, 1964).
15. Henry James, *What Maisie Knew* (New York, 1954), Preface, p. xi–xii.
16. Roth, *Call It Sleep*, p. 441.

now turn to the apprehension of childhood that belongs to him alone. We have placed James in the tradition of Hawthorne, Dickens, Carroll, and Mark Twain, authors who saw in the child and the theme of childhood a "convenient image" through which to express their feelings about the age in which they lived. Like Hawthorne, James recognized the possibility of evil in the child; like Dickens, he saw in the child a means of articulating his protest against that which he found disturbing in his society, and like Carroll and Twain, he sensed the isolation and bewilderment of the child in an incomprehensible adult world. Because James understood that ambiguity is intrinsic to human experience, because he viewed it as an inevitable concomitant of the human state, he was able to explore the child with extraordinary modernity. He sensed the contradictions of childhood, observed the coexistence of good and evil in the child, and dramatized its search for identity and moral purpose.

James's feeling that childhood is a time of unhappiness dominated his treatment of children in every phase of his development as a writer. His early critical appraisals of contemporary fellow-novelists exhibit an awareness of, and concern with, the way children were being presented in fiction. His resistance to the prevailing sentimentality and "the cult of the child" in literature was forceful and consistent. It is true that his own early fictional children are pathetic, unknowing, passive pawns in an evil adult game, but their function is not to elicit puerile responses from the reader; it is rather to illuminate the ironic aspects of adult hypocrisy and corruption. James was a man of his age as well as an unusually perceptive observer of men and manners. He was immersed in the life of his time and reacted sensitively to the currents of thought that prevailed during his lifetime. It comes as no surprise, then, to learn that in his treatment of children he traveled the same road from simplicity to complexity as did other distinguished novelists of his day. But his complexity carried him further, bringing him closer, indeed, to the era of Freud and modern psychology than any of his predecessors or contemporaries.

CHAPTER II

The Apprentice Stories

Mrs. Humphrey Ward recalled that "Mr. James [was not] an indiscriminate lover of children; he was not normally much at home with them, though *always* good to them. But the childish instinct had in fact divined the profound tenderness and chivalry which were the very root of his nature." [1] Hugh Walpole remembered walking with James in fields near Rye. Two small children opened a gate for them and James took out some coppers, but he talked so volubly and for such a long time that they took flight in terror. Walpole says that James "stood, bewildered, the pennies in his hand. What had he done? What had he said? He had meant nothing but kindness. . . . He was greatly distressed, going over every possible corner of it in his mind. He alluded to it for days afterwards." Muriel Draper recounts how James frightened her little boy by the intensity with which he concentrated on the buttons on the child's jacket. James had meant only to be playful. Yet in some instances, James's sensitivity and genuine feeling of sympathy for children managed to communicate itself. "He was serious with children," observed G. K. Chesterton, "I saw a little boy gravely present him with a crushed and dirty dandelion. He bowed; but did not smile." Mrs. Joseph Conrad related the following: "Our small boy . . . hated to be nursed by strangers. Mr. Henry James at once took him on his knee and forgot his existence, now and then giving him an absent-minded squeeze while talking to Conrad. We expected a petulant protest and a determined wriggle to get away, but the child's tact,

1. Mrs. Ward's reminiscences as well as those that follow are from Simon Nowell-Smith, *The Legend of the Master* (New York, 1948), pp. 90–91.

his instinctive sense of Henry James's personality, surpassed our highest expectations. He sat perfectly resigned and still for more than half an hour till Mr. James released him with a kiss."

In spite of such feelings of constraint, James closely observed children and had striking insight into their states of being from the first. In 1866, when he was twenty three, he reviewed *Winifred Bertram and the World She Lived In,* by Mrs. E. R. Charles, whose heroine is a child-paragon, pious and charitable. In the course of his appraisal, James made these observations:

We firmly believe that children in pinafores, however rich their natural promise, do not indulge in extemporaneous prayer, in the cognition of Scripture texts, and in the visitation of the poor and needy, except in very conscious imitation of their elders. The best good they accomplish is effected through a compromise with their essentially immoral love of pleasure. To be disinterested is among the very latest lessons they learn, and we should look with suspicion upon a little girl whose life was devoted to the service of an idea. In other words, children grow positively good only as they grow wise, and they grow wise only as they grow old and leave childhood behind them. To make them good before their time is to make them wise before their time, which is a very painful consummation.[2]

One of James's future themes—the association of the cognitive faculty with moral growth—is contained in this passage. In an age when the child was seen as a miniature adult, reflecting the virtues and vices of an adult world, James showed an understanding in advance of his time. Another significant observation was that "an habitually pre-occupied child is likely to be an unhappy one, and an unhappy one—although like Mr. Dickens's Little Nell, she may never do anything naughty—is certainly little more than an instrument of pathos. We can conceive of nothing more pernicious for a child than a premature sense of the seriousness of life. . . ." James's mature and sensitive portrait of a child—little Maisie Farange, of *What Maisie Knew*—would dramatize this early insight into the emotional life of the child.

2. Henry James, *Notes and Reviews* (Cambridge, Mass., 1921), pp. 149–50.

Young James's intuitive grasp of the true experience of childhood determined, to a degree, his critical response to the prevailing sentimental view in fiction. The fledgling author had definite ideas about the role of children and the theme of childhood in literature. "We are utterly weary of stories about precocious little girls," he wrote in 1865, "In the first place, they are in themselves disagreeable and unprofitable objects of study; and in the second, they are always the precursors of a not less unprofitable middle-aged lover."[3] The occasion for this unequivocal pronouncement was a review of Louisa M. Alcott's then-current novel, *Moods*. The arbitrary nature of such a statement can, in part, be attributed to the twenty-two-year-old critic's impulse to attack a kind of fiction that had become highly acceptable to established editors and publishers of the day. The aristocratic, intuitively charitable and (by virtue of its breeding) benevolent infant was enjoying unprecedented success. Of this portrait James said, "Nothing would tend more to make a child insufferably arrogant than the constant presence of a company of pensioners of its own bounty. Children are essentially democratic, and to represent the poor as in a state of perpetual dependence on them is to destroy some of their happiest traits."[4]

For James, even in those early years, a specious fictional rendering of any aspect of life was an immoral act. Reviewing *The Gayworthys: A Story of Threads and Thrums*, by Mrs. A. D. J. Whitney, he noted that "its [the novel's] radical defect is the degradation of sentiment by making children responsible for it. This practice is becoming the bane of our novels . . . it is, in our opinion, as fatal to the dignity of serious feeling and to the grandeur of strong passions as the most flagrant immoralities of French fiction. Heaven defend us from the puerile!"[5] It was inevitable that a writer who was to place emphasis on the cognitive faculty of his fictional characters—who was, in fact, to measure their moral worth in terms of their intellectual development—should denounce the sentimental genre.

3. Ibid., p. 50.
4. Ibid., p. 150.
5. Ibid., p. 95.

Just as some authors of his day sought to erase the differences between childhood and adult experience, so James endeavored to preserve this difference, to keep the two experiences separate and unique. "A man's childhood and his manhood," he wrote, "can never, without a violation of truth, be made the same story; much less may the youth and maturity of a woman. . . ." [6] In 1865, James shared the classical attitude toward children and the theme of childhood in literature. The child, because innocent and immature, was not appropriate subject matter for serious literary treatment. "There are, of course, few things so charming as the innocence of childhood, just as there are few things so interesting as the experience of manhood. But they cannot in a love-story be successfully combined." [7] It was not, in fact, until many years later in 1887 that James was to concede—in his tribute to Robert Louis Stevenson—that to be absorbed in the "delightful period" of childhood could be a "sufficient philosophy" for certain novelists. [8] At twenty-two, James reflected an interest in the adult world which for him was the supreme subject of the novelist. He discerned the danger that sentimentality posed to fiction and that to endow children with adult attributes was one way of perverting art. He did not hesitate to criticize those novelists who sacrificed verisimilitude in order to appeal to the primitive feelings of the reader. In the light of these incisive comments on children, let us see how the novelist himself sketched his children in his early fiction.

It can be said at once that James's critical remarks about children in literature are more substantial and illuminating during this period than is his presentation of them in his stories. Between 1864 and 1868, the novelist adhered to his stated view that children have no significant place in adult fiction. Yet a child does appear from time to time, always with a clearly defined function in the story. Indeed James's first published tale, "A Tragedy of Error," has a child in it. This anonymous tale first ap-

6. Ibid., p. 96.
7. Ibid., p. 96.
8. Henry James, *Partial Portraits* (London, 1919), p. 144.

peared in a New York journal, *The Continental Monthly*, in February of 1864. Its heroine, Hortense Bernier, is involved in a love affair during her husband's absence overseas on business. Desperate over his impending return, she seeks out a ruthless boatman and plots with him to have her husband drowned. The boatman will meet the vessel beyond the breakwater and offer to row her husband ashore. M. Bernier is lame; it will be easy for the boatman to drown him.

When Hortense goes to the quay, she is first attracted to the boatman because she is witness to a scene between him and a small child. The man is sitting on the steps of the landing place smoking his pipe when the child, carry-a jug of milk, passes. The boatman calls out in a brutal tone and "the little child look[s] back, but, instead of obeying, only quicken[s] its walk." After being roundly cursed by the boatman, "the child stopped, and ruefully made its way to its relative, looking around several times toward the house, as if to appeal to some counter authority." The helplessness of the child in the face of the adult's bullying is clearly delineated. When the boatman lunges toward the child to take possession of the jug of milk, the child makes "no answer. It simply and vainly endeavor[s] to twist its neck around under the man's gripe, and transmit some call for succor to the house." Possessed of the jug, the man drains it while the child quietly watches him, with a steady gaze of rebuke for the boatman's inhumanity:

The child, although liberated, did not retreat. It stood watching its uncle drink until he lowered the jug. Then, as he met its eyes, it said, "It was for the baby."
For the moment the man was irresolute. But the child seemed to have a foresight of the parental resentment, for it had hardly spoken when it darted backward and scampered off, just in time to elude a blow from the jug, which the man sent clattering at its heels. When it was out of sight, he faced about to the water again . . . with a heavy scowl and a murmur that sounded to Madame Bernier very like—"I wish the baby'd choke." [9]

9. Henry James, *The Complete Tales of Henry James*, ed. Leon Edel (New York, 1962), I, 30–31.

Here indeed was a man worthy of the task Hortense Bernier had in mind for him.

The obvious reason for the introduction of this vivid episode is to justify Hortense's choice of the boatman for the murder. James, however, achieves more than this bit of motivation. The introduction of the incident leaves his heroine somehow less culpable. The fact that she properly evaluates the boatman implies a recognition on her part of her own depravity. An awareness of her own wickedness is a difficult thing to live with. Knowledge of evil is impossible without perception of good. The boatman seems unaware of his own malevolence. He represents brute force. Hortense Bernier, in recognizing the malignity of the man, proves that she knows that good exists and that, in following her course of action, she is renouncing it. James clearly wants us to be moved by her plight for toward the end of the scene with the boatman, after she has revealed her plan, Hortense cries out "O God!" and her behavior at that moment is described in the following way:

Madame Bernier sprang up in her seat, threw out her arms, and sank down again, burying her face in her knees. Her companion hastily shipped his oars, and laid his hands on her shoulders.
"*Allons donc*, in the devil's name, don't break down," said he; "we'll come to an understanding." (*Complete Tales*, I, 41)

The boatman, who has no conception of evil, misinterprets her behavior. He believes that she is upset because he may not do the deed for her. Afraid of losing his reward, he assures her that she can count on him. Hortense, however, is reacting as a woman of feeling, aware of the wrongdoing on which she is embarked. She does indeed, as Leon Edel has remarked, foreshadow in a crude and primitive way James's later "bad heroines."

A child does not appear in James's tales until three years after "A Tragedy of Error." In 1867 "My Friend Bingham" was published in the March issue of the *Atlantic Monthly*. (*Complete Tales*, I, 165) In this little-known tale, the narrator goes to a seaside resort with his close friend, George Bingham. During a stroll by the sea, they become aware of a young woman walking on the sand with a sickly child. They conjecture that she must be spending the autumn at the seashore in the interest of the child's health. One afternoon, when the two friends are out duck-hunting, Bingham inadvertently shoots and kills the child. In the process of trying to make amends to the bereaved mother, Bingham falls in love with her; she returns his feeling, and after a decent interval, they marry and are presumed to live happily ever after.

Clearly the child in "My Friend Bingham" is there as "trigger" to the dramatic action. The infant and the circumstances surrounding its death form the basis for the subsequent events. While in "A Tragedy of Error" the child added feeling and tone, thus indirectly contributing to the complexity of the central character, in "My Friend Bingham" it is essential to the sequence of events. The child does not, however, exist as a character; it is rather a contrivance in the story. The sickly, passive little victim of a stray bullet, unknowing and unknown, does not even have a name and is referred to always as "the child." At this point in his development, James is still using the child to evoke feelings of tenderness in the reader and as a plot device. Nevertheless there is an aspect of this tale which is of great importance in the light of the author's subsequent treatment of childhood. In "My Friend Bingham" we observe the first intimation of a motif that was to recur in James's novels and tales with striking regularity—that of the "sacrificial" child. In certain stories James's children are an impediment to adult relationships and are frequently killed off in order that adults may fulfill themselves. As the novelist's children took on identity, the sacrificial youngsters became predominently male. Somehow little boys had to be gotten rid of in James. This early tale prefigures the characteristic Jamesian fantasy that would be more fully treated in "The Author of Beltraffio," "The Pupil," and "The Turn of the Screw."

A little more than a year after "My Friend Bingham," a child figures once more in "A Problem," which appeared in the June issue of the *Galaxy*, 1868. (*Complete Tales*, I, 369) As in the earlier tales, the child has no individualized personality. In this tale James makes a more concentrated effort than hitherto to engage the sympathy of the reader by appealing directly to the traditional association of childhood with feelings of pathos and tenderness. The pathetic little girl "came out of the cruel embrace of disease, panting and exhausted, but uninjured." The mother watches "the faint glow of returning life in its poor little wasted cheeks." And when the father plays with the child, "the baby softly open[s] her eyes, and, vaguely conscious of her father, lift[s] her hand and languidly clutch[es] his nose." Finally, just before the denouement, at the child's funeral, the father "bow[s] to the clergyman, and [goes to look] at the little remnant of mortality which had once been his daughter."

The child in James's fiction had yet to acquire a defined personality; however, in this tale we are made to feel her presence and to respond more subjectively to her unhappy fate. Yet again the infant in this tale serves as a contrivance for furthering the dramatic action. The prophecy about the child leads to the revelation of a second prophecy. This, in turn, creates the "problem" of the tale; it is solved only when the original prophecy is fulfilled. The idea of the child, her evocative image, becomes pivotal to the events; the child herself remains in the background. The theme of the sacrificed child is more clearly stated in "A Problem" than in "My Friend Bingham." Through the death of the innocent child, the parents are reunited. No stray bullet ended the unhappy little girl's life; some evil and undefinable force determined her sad destiny. It would appear as though, for James, parents and children could not live comfortably together in the same fictional world and most often the child is expendable.

The youngster in "Osborne's Revenge," published in the *Galaxy*, July, 1868, (*Complete Tales*, II, 13) continues to affect plot development. It is introduced to bring about a meeting between two leading characters. The situation foreshadows the one in "Daisy Miller," when Winterbourne encounters Daisy through her talkative brother. No better example of James's growth as a painter of children is needed than a comparison of Randolph C. Miller with the child of this early tale. James could, doubtless, have used some other agent for bringing about the necessary meeting between the two principal characters. None, however, would have achieved so felicitously the pictorial effect he sought in "Osborne's Revenge." James frequently used visual art devices in his fiction. He habitually "saw" a scene as a landscape or figures arranged. Osborne's first meeting with the child illustrates the author's tendency to graphically capture and "frame" a scene through careful presentation of descriptive detail:

On a broad flat rock, at about a dozen yards from the shore, stood a child of some five years—a handsome boy, fair-haired and well dressed—stamping his feet and wringing his hands in an apparent agony of terror. It was easy to understand the situation. The child had ventured out on the rock while the water was still low, and had become so much absorbed in paddling with his little wooden spade among the rich marine deposits on its surface, that he had failed to observe the advance of the waves, which now completely covered the intermediate fragments of rock and were foaming and weltering betwixt him and the shore. The poor little fellow stood screaming to the winds and the waters, and quite unable to answer Osborne's shouts of interrogation and comfort. (*Complete Tales*, II, 22)

After Osborne rescues the child and returns him to his aunt, Henrietta, the compositional center shifts to her. The young woman, her arms around the child, her face expressing terror at what might have happened, takes on the aspect of a charming *tableau vivant*. The picture is not only aesthetically satisfying; it is thematically significant as well. The possible consequences of Henrietta Congreve's momentary neglect of her young charge occasions her chagrin, and so her face becomes "flushed," her eyes "flash," and "the flashes [melt] into a couple of tears." James has created a beguiling image of femininity to ensnare a young man destined to become hopelessly beguiled. The child adds immeasurably to the finished canvas. By presenting the incident pictorially, the author intensifies the feeling of the moment, reinforces the theme of the tale.

"Osborne's Revenge" is the last tale in which the child

figures merely as pictorial embellishment or technical expedient. Subsequent children will have more significant functions and more individualized personalities. The romantic tendency to focus on the child as a unique entity, however, will be tempered in James by his devotion to the truthful reconstruction of human experience. The child will acquire increasing significance only in relation to the central themes of his later fiction. Although the population of children in the tales of the 1860's is sparse, those who do appear give evidence of the young author's dedication to his craft. In these early tales children are carefully "placed," cautiously used; any appeal on their behalf is nearly always made by indirection and is primarily aimed at rendering the traditional place of children and nursery within an adult world.

CHAPTER III

The "Spoiled" Child

James was increasingly to be preoccupied with the quality of the child's experience and the implications of this experience for its future development. The tales of his first mature period (the 1870's) and of his middle period (the 1880's) give evidence of the novelist's growing interest in the significance of childhood impressions and their role in the formation of character. These stories demonstrate that the maturing novelist recognized the malleability of the young. He felt that their "helpless plasticity" demanded a sense of responsibility on the part of those answerable to them. It can be said that during these years a definite theory of education was beginning to take form for the novelist. James suggests in the tales of this period that adult dereliction—social as well as parental—could very well produce a generation of "spoiled" youngsters who would threaten the very fabric of society.

If the preponderance of James's criticism seems to be aimed at American parents, it is because children have for such a long time dominated the American social scene. It is generally accepted that children have played, and do play, a more significant role in the lives of the American adults who surround them than has been the case in other countries. We have long been, and are, a society that is dominated by, and caters almost exclusively to, the young. Americans tend to see in childhood the youth of their nation and in children the image of their own possibilities. Young people reflect our expectations even when they fall short of the ideal. The shallowness of American expectations and the absence of inner discipline which James observed at home and abroad disturbed him. In this country the necessities of life have, by and large, always been well in hand; the tendency has been to evaluate everything in terms of "the best that money can buy" and to place great emphasis on individual freedom of choice. This materialistic and unrestrained view, to the exclusion of other important values in child-rearing, moved James to protest in his fictional representations of American children and their parents. His criticism was by no means confined to the American social scene. The "prosaic little mortals" whom he observed on a visit to an English Workhouse in 1879 captured his imagination as fully as the raucous American imps he encountered in the lobbies of luxury hotels at home and abroad. The educational and emotional environment of all children, American and European, became the concern of the maturing author.

Significant in the tales of the 1870's and 1880's was the fresh view James took of the child-parent relationship. During the Victorian period little, if any, thought had been given to interaction between adult and child; if children did not behave as their elders thought they should, they were considered inherently deficient in moral worth. In England the evangelicals, and in America the Puritans, conceived of human nature as essentially base. The only guide to salvation lay in the scriptures literally interpreted, in strict adherence to a moral code as evidenced by acts of conscience. The mature individual sought salvation through piety and virtuous deeds. Children, as diminutive adults, would be expected to exhibit the same tendencies. If there was no qualitative difference between the fundamental aspirations of the child and the adult, then individual responsibility for good or evil rested squarely on the shoulders of children as it did on those of their elders. This attitude, which strongly affected English and American authors of the period, accounts, in part, for the numerous fictional representations of precocious infants performing acts of piety and charity for the good of their souls.

Equally salient was the influence of the Dickensian child who had left his imprint on British and American

literature of social protest. Both of these fictional portraits, the child as potential sinner and the child as sinned
against, are predicated on a common assumption that is
deterministic in its implications. The assumption is that
interaction between adult and child is of minor significance in seeking solutions to the problems being dealt
with. In one case responsibility rests with the child; in
the other it rests exclusively with the adult, and it is
incumbent upon him to effect change in social institutions
that exploit the child.

Henry James took a view of the child-adult relationship
which was at variance with the dominant trends of his
time. "The painter's subject," he said in his preface to
Roderick Hudson, "consist[s] ever, obviously, of the related state, to each other, of certain figures and things.
To exhibit these relations, once they have all been
recognized, is to 'treat' his idea, which involves neglecting
none of those that directly minister to interest." What
James stated explicitly in his preface of 1907 is implicit
in his treatment of child and parent in his tales of the
1870's and 1880's. These children respond to, are, in fact,
to a significant degree formed by, the attitudes, feelings,
and behavior of important adults in their lives.

In "Master Eustace," which appeared in the *Galaxy*,
November, 1871 (*Complete Tales*, II), James explores
the dramatic possibilities of a situation in which a guilty
mother tries to atone for her transgression by smothering
her child with affection. She convinces herself that "love,
love, pure love, is the sum and substance of maternal
duty, and that the love which reasons and requires and
refuses is cruel and wicked." The fact that James considered such a philosophy of child-rearing disastrous for
all concerned is evidenced by the tragic denouement.

Mrs. Garnyer, an attractive widow, hires a governess for
her small son, Eustace, and it is through the eyes of this
young woman that we watch the drama unfold. The
narrator-governess soon senses that her employer is hiding some secret sorrow; yet Mrs. Garnyer seems to live
only for her son. She envelopes him with affection,
anticipates his every wish, denies him nothing. Inevitably

he grows into a selfish, arrogant young man. James explores the relationship between mother and son in depth. He exposes with unusual finesse the mechanism behind the mother's "love," a love that is tinged with eroticism. The novelist has captured the quality of seduction in the mother's feeling for her son by carefully choosing the figurative language describing her behavior with him. She "would steal up behind him and kiss him softly on the forehead, as if to marry his sweet illusions to sweeter reality." The governess senses the symbiotic nature of their tie and reacts against this situation in which the mother, in order to satisfy her own needs, encourages the dependence and latent eroticism of the son. "For my part, I wanted to divorce them. It was a sad pity, I thought, that desire and occasion, in the lad's life, played so promptly into each other's hands. . . ." The mother plays the role of seductress; the son assumes the stance of a lover. Before leaving to go abroad, Eustace cautions his mother "not to be too cheerful, mind. You are not to forget me an instant. If you do I will never forgive you. I insist on being missed. There's little enough merit in loving me when I am here; I wish to be loved in my absence."

While Eustace is away, an old friend of his mother, Mr. Cope, arrives from India where he has been living for many years. It becomes evident to the narrator-governess that Mr. Cope holds the key to the mystery that surrounds Mrs. Garnyer. She conjectures that this gentleman must have been Mrs. Garnyer's first and only love, since it is made quite clear that she never loved her late husband; for some reason they could not marry; he left for India, broken-hearted, and she entered into a loveless marriage. This would explain why she lavished so much affection on her son. Mr. Cope probably married in India; his wife must have died recently and now he had returned to claim his first love. The fantasy appeals to the romantic governess. "For ten years I had been pitying Mrs. Garnyer; it was odd now to find myself envying her. Patient waiting is no loss, and at last her day had come." This envy may have prompted the governess to write Eustace

"full of praises of Mr. Cope" and "of his mother's im-
proved condition." In any event, after she posted the
letter, it occurred to her that she had been precipitate.
She doubts "whether, even amid the larger life of the
grand tour, he [Eustace] had unlearned the old trick of
jealousy." Her concern is justified. Mrs. Garnyer and Mr.
Cope, perhaps intuiting danger, marry while Eustace is
away. They have not, unfortunately, reckoned with the
effects of Mrs. Garnyer's creed of "love" vis-à-vis her son.
Eustace returns and, upon being told of the marriage,
reacts with a fury that exceeds normal bounds. In his
repugnance at the notion of his mother's wedded state
there is an echo of Hamlet, but Eustace is quite explicit
as to the source of his revulsion:

> "*Married!*" the poor boy shouted, "MARRIED, you say!" He
> turned deadly pale, and stood staring at me with his mouth
> wide open . . . "Without me—without notice—without shame!
> . . . What has come to her? Is she mad? Has she lost her head,
> her heart, her memory—all that made her mine? . . . Her
> husband! And I—I—I—what has she done with me? Where am
> I in this devil's game? . . . She has insulted me—dishonored
> me. . . . Am I a man to be made light of? Brought up as a
> flower and trampled as a weed! Wrapped in cotton and then
> exposed. . . ." (*Complete Tales,* II, 366)

Despite the melodrama, the scene moves because James
reveals the wellspring of Eustace's wrath. On one level,
the most obvious, the young man is the selfish product
of an overly permissive and indulgent parent, but on
another and deeper level, he is the victim of feelings for
his mother which have no rational basis and which he is
at a loss to identify. These are the feelings that have been
"wrapped in cotton" and are now "exposed." His mother
has, in effect, destroyed his manhood. "You see an angry
man," says Eustace, "an outraged man, but a man, mind
you! He means to act as one." In his frustration Eustace
throws to the floor the pearl necklace he has bought for
his mother and leaves it "ground into fragments on the
carpet as if by his boot-heels." Thus the pearl, traditional
symbol of feminine purity, is violated by the "outraged
man." He leaves the house in a fury. When the governess
enters his wildly disordered room, she finds that "his

father's relics [are] standing in a row, untouched, on the mantel-shelf, save for a couple of pistols, mounted with his initials, in silver, which were tossed upon the table." The pistols figure as an emblem of his manhood as well as a device for effecting the melodramatic ending of the tale.

When Eustace's mother cries out that she married for the sake of his happiness, he flings back at her, "Is my happiness in a ruined home—in a disputed heart—in a bullying stepfather! You have chosen him big and strong! Cry your eyes out—you are no mother of mine." Eustace cannot abide the blow to his masculinity his mother's marriage signifies for him. Having been secure in his role of the only man in her life, he is suddenly confronted with the fact that he has been displaced by another who is "big and strong," one who will assume in reality the masculine role the boy had assigned to himself in fantasy. Mrs. Garnyer senses the irrational aspect of Eustace's behavior and cries out, "He's ill, he's mad—he doesn't know what he says . . . look at him, soothe him, cure him . . . Eustace, Eustace, be cured!"

Eustace's denunciation of his mother quite literally breaks her heart. She is helped to her room and, as she lies dying, she recognizes the destruction she has caused: "It's my fault—all, all, all! I heaped up folly on folly and weakness on weakness. My heart's broken; it will never be of any use again. You have been right, my dear—I perverted him, I taught him to strike. Oh what a blow! He's hard—he's hard. He's cruel. He has no heart. He is blind with vanity and egotism." (*Complete Tales*, II, 370)

She has understood finally that "love" is not enough for a child, that guidance and firmness and a sense of values are indispensable. She sees as well, that her love had its roots in guilt, for it turns out that Eustace is an illegitimate child, the fruit of her affair of twenty years ago with Mr. Cope. Love born of guilt, the poor woman realizes, is no love at all. In the last moments of her life, Mrs. Garnyer must face the fact that love can have its pathological aspects. "I don't want to live," she murmured, "I have seen something too dreadful. It could

never be patched up; we should never be the same. He has shown his character—isn't it his character? It's bad!" The question that Mrs. Garnyer asks is pathetic in its helplessness. For she too is faced with questions she cannot answer and irrational feelings only dimly perceived. She sees but does not see; she senses but does not really comprehend the extent of the damage she has unconsciously done.

While the young James of "Master Eustace" exhibits a flare for the melodramatic the older James would eschew, the tale has elements that are characteristic of the novelist at his best. His main emphasis is on the development of an ugly character in a spoiled child. It is Eustace and the forces that shaped him which are James's primary concern. His rendering of Eustace is arresting because of the depth of psychological perception the author brings to bear on the character. The victim of an environment that perpetuated an unhealthy dependence on his mother, Eustace is driven, by feelings he cannot identify, to destroy all that has meaning for him. As James develops his character, he reveals a mature grasp of the complexities of human behavior as well as consummate skill in psychological portraiture. The narrator's first encounter with the little boy reveals that the foundation for future problems has already been laid by the mother's fond hand:

The boy from his early childhood presented himself as a little man who would take a line of his own. He was not one who would ever wait for things, good or evil; he would snatch boldly at the one sort and snap his fingers at the other. He had a pale, dark skin, not altogether healthy in tone; a mass of fine brown hair, which seemed given him just to emphasize by its dancing sweep, the petulant little nods and shakes of his head; and a deep, wilful, malicious eye. His eye told me from the first that I should have no easy work with him, and with every possible relaxation of the nursery-code my place never became in the least a sinecure. (*Complete Tales*, II, 343)

Later we are told that "Eustace had a particular fancy for the moon, for everything bright and inaccessible and absurd." From the first Eustace desired what he could never hope to have and the course of his emotional development was inevitable. With this remarkable, if admittedly flamboyant, characterization of Eustace, James illuminated another aspect of that most complex of human emotions, "love." The multileveled view of Eustace's relationship with his mother saves the tale from becoming the mundane story of an over-indulged child. The boy has been "spoiled," but James has given the term an added dimension and increased significance. At the end of the tale, having learned of his origin, Eustace tries to shoot himself with his father's pistol. "It is not murder," says Mr. Cope, "but it has just missed being suicide. It has been fatal only to the looking glass. The mirror was shivered." Knowledge of his illegitimacy shatters Eustace's image of himself just as his mother's marriage called into question his masculinity; he is not able to sustain the psychic wounds. In the last line of the tale the narrator tells us that "the son Eustace was forgiven—the father Mr. Cope never." Thus Master Eustace emerges as victim and victimizer, his mother as slayer and slain, and James demonstrates once more that parent and child cannot live together in one world.

The maturing artist, however, has recognized that a realistic representation of life must take into account the effect that one personality will have on the fate of another, what George Eliot in *Middlemarch* called "the stealthy convergence of human lots." Children are profoundly affected by the adults in their lives and the adults cannot blame fate, the gods, or supernatural forces for that which their own dereliction brings about.

James's response to the idea of childhood was at this time essentially romantic but his treatment of children in his early fiction was classical; in his later work he moved toward realism. Fundamentally he conceived of the child as possessing "the sweet, shy bloom of ideal infancy." [1] An environment that tended to disturb this ideal state invited censure of the most stringent kind. In the case of Master Eustace it was misguided compensatory love rooted in guilt and corruption which

1. Henry James, *Literary Reviews and Essays*, ed. Albert Mordell (New York, 1957), p. 245.

robbed the child of its due. There were to be other ways of "spoiling" children and they would all depend, in some measure, on parental deficiency. In each case there would be an absence of clearly defined values on the part of thoughtless or unconcerned adults. There is often evidence of the failure of perception and an inability to provide a standard of behavior by those who are figures of authority.

In 1875 James was concerned with the failure of many American parents to establish appropriate rapport with their children, to provide them with precepts that would serve as guideposts in the conduct of their lives. The theme is fully explored in "Daisy Miller." Both Daisy and her precocious little brother, Randolph, stand as a rebuke to parents who are remiss in their obligation to their children. "Daisy Miller" was, in part, James's response to a situation of which he was aware and to which he reacted with some intensity. His concern is reflected in a review of Louisa M. Alcott's *Eight Cousins: or Aunt Hill* (1875): "It is sometimes affirmed by the observant foreigner, on visiting these shores . . . that American children are without a certain charm usually possessed by the youngsters of the Old World. The little girls are apt to be pert and shrill, the little boys to be aggressive and knowing." [2]

The criticism, still being made by foreign visitors to these shores, impelled James to seek out the cause of the national differences and, having found the root of the problem, to comment on it in his fiction. What were Americans doing to their children to produce the affluent urchins who occasioned such adverse comment from European observers? His remarks in a literary review of the period—always such a fruitful source for James's opinions on children and child-rearing—offer a partial answer:

The smart satirical tone is the last one in the world to be used in describing to children their elders and betters and the social mysteries that surround them. Miss Alcott seems to have a private understanding with the youngsters she depicts,

2. Ibid.

at the expense of their pastors and masters; and her idea of friendliness to the infant generation seems to be . . . to initiate them into the humorous view of them taken by their elders when the children are out of the room . . . All this is both poor entertainment and poor instruction. What children want is the objective, as the philosophers say; it is good for them to feel that people and things around them that appeal to their respect are beautiful and powerful specimens of what they seem to be.[3]

It would appear that Americans had to go through the agonies and suffer the results of the grossly misunderstood and indiscriminately applied methods of "progressive" child-rearing in the 1930's, 40's, and 50's in order to appreciate the validity of James's observation of 1875. Children without guidance, standards, and objects of authority they can respect are lost little souls. James felt this to be true and his "spoiled" children of the 70's, 80's and 90's are not an indictment of them but a dramatization of their plight.

One wonders why critics have been so quick to remark upon the appalling aspects of Randolph C. Miller of "Daisy Miller" (*Complete Tales*, IV) without perceiving his pathetic side. If, as F. W. Dupee contends, Randolph is "the precious American 'bad boy' done for once in acids," he is also a "pale" and lonely little nine-year-old who has "a voice immature, and yet, somehow, not young," a child who "does not sleep very much," and whose teeth are falling out from overindulgence in sweets. Randolph is more than a figure of satire; he is touching. Like his flighty sister and his ineffectual mother, the boy lives in a social and moral vacuum committed to nothing and no one. These voids are evils in James's world, and it is noteworthy that in singling out the materialism and a lack of commitment as detrimental to the character and emotional health of the young child, James was well in advance of his time.

An environment in which aesthetic appreciation and the exercise of the intellect are valued above discipline and guidance was, in James's view, far from ideal. His comments on the absence of these stabilizing factors in

3. Ibid., pp. 245–46.

his own childhood, as expressed in his autobiography, *A Small Boy and Others,* attest his conviction that clearly defined limits are indispensable for psychic growth. But, an anarchic environment in which ignorance and vulgarity obscure all thought and sensitivity was unbearable to him. He dramatized both cases in his fiction. Isabel Archer, in *The Portrait of a Lady,* reaps the tragic consequences of freedom undefined, against a background of vague aesthetic and cultural aspirations; Daisy and Randolph Miller are the victims of an equally vague freedom without any recognizable frame of reference, but the vulgarity and materialism surrounding them leave their situation with no redeeming feature.

Armed against life with nothing but his alpenstock, "the sharp point of which he thrust[s] into everything that he approach[es]—the flower-beds, the garden benches, the trains of the ladies' dresses," Randolph is living an aimless, joyless childhood and faces an equally undirected and purposeless adulthood. Never disciplined by his mother or his sister, without benefit of his father's presence, he is a child adrift and with an ambiguous future. His recurrent wish to quit Europe and return to Schenectady reflects his need for a port in the storm, some place where he can feel he belongs, where he will have a clearly defined and comprehensible set of values by which he can live. He hates Europe "worse and worse every day!" The best place he has seen is the American ship that brought them to Europe, the *City of Richmond,* "only it was turned the wrong way." What the child is pleading for, what his irritative behavior masks, is the need for some stability in his little life which will give it boundaries and direction. James's portrait of Randolph reveals not that the novelist loathed American children but that he felt deep compassion for them and profound resentment toward those who treated the responsibility of parenthood lightly.

The question of parental love and its role in the life and education of the child retained its hold on James's imagination during these years. In *Washington Square,* published in 1880, James examined the obverse of all-enveloping love; he dramatized the effect of parental hostility on the sensitive nature of a young girl.

Catherine Sloper, the "plain," undistinguished daughter of the clever and distinguished Dr. Sloper, was destined from birth to disappoint and frustrate her father. His first-born, a son, had died in infancy; shortly after Catherine's birth, he lost his beautiful and charming wife. Dr. Sloper never gave his little girl an opportunity to help fill the void: "Mrs. Sloper gave birth to a second infant—an infant of a sex which rendered the poor child, to the Doctor's sense, an inadequate substitute for his lamented first-born, of whom he had promised himself to make an admirable man. The little girl was a disappointment; but this was not the worst. A week after her birth the young mother . . . suddenly betrayed alarming symptoms, and before another week had elapsed Austin Sloper was a widower." [4]

James presents Dr. Sloper with remarkable psychological insight. The effect of the father's attitude on the daughter's development as a woman is rendered with absolute clarity. Dr. Sloper masks his hostility with a so-called "realistic" evaluation of his "plain," "dull" daughter's chances for happiness in life. So diligent is he in the performance of his "duty" that he eventually saves his daughter from a fortune-hunter as well as from the only joy she was ever to know. The Doctor is nothing if not "responsible" in his role of parent: "It must not be supposed that Dr. Sloper visited his disappointment upon the poor girl, or ever let her suspect that she had played him a trick. On the contrary, for fear of being unjust to her, he did his duty with exemplary zeal, and recognized that she was a faithful and affectionate child." (*Washington Square*, p. 90)

If Mrs. Garnyer destroyed Eustace with "love," Dr. Sloper achieved the same with "duty." In his rendering of the Doctor, however, James presents us with a more complex character study. He has included the subtle shadings that constitute a fully realized portrait of a

---

4. Henry James, *Selected Fiction*, ed. Leon Edel (New York, 1953), p. 83.

powerful, intelligent, and unconsciously virulent father. James endows Dr. Sloper with a sardonic air, a kind of "humor" devastating to the sensitive, shy, deeply responsive Catherine. In her eagerness to please, to somehow make up for her "deficiencies," she tends to over-dress, and when the Doctor sees her at a ball in a rather tasteless crimson gown, he makes the most of the moment:

> "Is it possible that this magnificent person is my child?" . . . You would have surprised him if you had told him so; but it is a literal fact that he almost never addressed his daughter save in the ironical form. Whenever he addressed her he gave her pleasure; but she had to cut her pleasure out of the pieces, as it were. There were portions left over, light remnants and snippets of irony, which she never knew what to do with, which seemed too delicate for her own use. . . . "I am not magnificent," she said, mildly, wishing she had put on another dress. "You are sumptuous, opulent, expensive," her father rejoined. "You look as if you had eighty thousand a year." (*Washington Square*, p. 102)

James was aware of aggression that so often lies behind the sardonic quip, the witty remark, and in Catherine's response to her father's latent hostility he projects the pain and bewilderment that such humor can bring to a docile and affectionate nature.

In his use of physical setting as a correlation to inner states of feeling in *Washington Square*, James prefigures the technical virtuosity he was to display in the novels of his major phase. Dr. Sloper takes Catherine to Europe so that she will forget Morris Townsend who wants to marry her for her money. After a year abroad, the Doctor senses that Catherine's feeling for Morris is unchanged. He is furious at not having succeeded in his plan. He finally confronts her in a lonely pass in the Alps. The novelist uses an arresting series of images to evoke a sense of Dr. Sloper's hatred and Catherine's dim perception of it:

> It was late in the afternoon, in the last of August; night was coming on, and as they had reached a great elevation, the air was cold and sharp. In the west there was a great suffusion of cold red light, which made the sides of the little valley look only the more rugged and dusky . . . [he] came close to her, as if he had something to say. He stopped in front of her, and stood looking at her with eyes that had kept the light of the

flushing snow-summits on which they had just been fixed. (*Washington Square*, pp. 217–18)

Dr. Sloper's feeling for his daughter is "cold" and "sharp," and, like the cold red light that suffuses the west, his anger at Catherine's struggle for a place in the sun engulfs them both. He asks her whether she has given Townsend up, and when she answers that it is not possible for her to stop loving Morris, the Doctor's true feelings for his daughter are revealed. Catherine becomes acutely aware of the force of his antipathy for her:

> She wondered what he meant—whether he wished to frighten her. If he did, the place was well chosen: this hard, melancholy dell, abandoned by the summer light, made her feel her loneliness. She looked around her, and her heart grew cold; for a moment her fear was great. . . . Had he brought her there on purpose, and was it part of a plan? . . . was it to startle her suddenly into a retraction—to take advantage of her by dread? Dread of what? The place was ugly and lonely, but the place could do her no harm. There was a kind of still intensity about her father which made him dangerous, but Catherine hardly went so far as to say to herself that it might be part of his plan to fasten his hand—the neat, fine, supple hand of a distinguished physician—in her throat. (*Washington Square*, pp. 218–19)

For the first time she confronts her father's aggressiveness. Catherine accepts the inevitability of it with admirable strength. She later tells Morris, "He is not very fond of me. . . . I felt it, in England, just before he came away. . . . He can't help it; we can't govern our affections . . . it's because he is so fond of my mother, whom we lost so long ago. She was beautiful, and very, very brilliant; he is always thinking of her. I am not at all like her." The girl's vague apprehensions, the impressions she could not define, the feelings she could not identify, fall into a describable pattern. Her belief in Morris Townsend's devotion gives her strength to accept the truth. When he fails her, Catherine withdraws into a protective shell of resignation; her capacity to love and be loved has been destroyed. In this work which James considered "too slight" to include in his New York Edition, the novelist has created a moving drama of parental cruelty and the way this can permanently damage a life.

The view of Henry James as somber moralist and as
stern critic of parental dereliction is in need of a correc-
tive lest we overemphasize one aspect of a writer who was
nothing if not diversified in his representation of life.
James had a delightful sense of humor, a fact often lost
sight of in pursuit of levels of meaning in his fiction. His
irony is not always tragic, and human absurdities, which
constitute a large part of human experience, did not
escape his keen observer's eye. If Randolph C. Miller
was pathetic, he was also "sassy" and amusingly (if un-
comfortably) familiar. To James, who was prone to
consider both sides of his coin, humor could indicate
seriousness of purpose as effectively as the absence of it.
Disturbing as their plight may be, there is, after all,
something comic in those tyrannical infants.

In "The Point of View," published in the *Century
Magazine*, December, 1882, (*Complete Tales*, IV) our
author looks at American children from the amusingly
outraged point of view of an anglicized American spin-
ster who has returned to these shores after spending
many years abroad. Her remarks are as lucid as they are
prophetic of the "juvenile takeover" that was to characterize our culture. The tale consists of eight letters written
by various visitors to America recording their impressions
of the country and its people. James is obviously enjoying
himself as he comments, through his characters, on the
differences in manners, mores, and expectations of these
foreign observers. One of the letters is from Miss Sturdy
whose name was aptly chosen. She describes herself as
"fifty years old—single, stout, and red in the face." But
she is cultivated, intelligent, perceptive, alive to the
humor of a situation. What she has to say about American children is strikingly contemporary in the twentieth
century. She speaks for herself, and I suspect for James,
on the tyranny of children in our society:

> *A propos* of the young people, that is our other danger; the
> young people are eating us up—there is nothing in America
> but young people. The country is made for the rising genera-
> tion; life is arranged for them; they are the destruction of
> society. People talk of them, consider them, defer to them,
> bow down to them. They are always present, and whenever

they are present there is an end to everything else. They are often very pretty; and physically, they are wonderfully looked after; they are scoured and brushed, they wear hygienic clothes, they go every week to the dentist's. But little boys kick your shins, and the little girls offer to slap your face! There is an immense literature entirely addressed to them, in which the kicking of shins and the slapping of faces is much recommended. As a woman of fifty I protest. I insist on being judged by my peers. It's too late, however, for several millions of little feet are actively engaged in stamping out conversation, and I don't see how long they can fail to keep it under. The future is theirs; maturity will evidently be at an increasing discount. Longfellow wrote a charming little poem, called "The Children's Hour," but he ought to have called it "The Children's Century." And by children, of course, I don't mean simple infants; I mean everything of less than twenty. The social importance of the young American increases steadily up to that age, and then suddenly it stops. (*Complete Tales*, IV, 487–88)

We who are daily advised through various media to "think young" by drinking a designated beverage, or those of us who, having reached the age of thirty, are admonished to "rush right out" to the nearest cosmetician to find ways of hiding the shameful fact, will, I think, appreciate Miss Sturdy's observations.

In the same tale James remarks, through the eyes of an English member of parliament, the acute feelings of nostalgia that children as a class seem to evoke in Americans:

My leading impression is that children in this country are better educated than the adults. The position of a child is, on the whole, one of great distinction. There is a popular ballad of which the refrain, if I am not mistaken, is "Make me a child again, just for to-night!" and which seems to express the sentiment of regret for lost privileges. At all events they are a powerful and independent class, and have organs, of immense circulation, in the press. They are often extremely "bright." (*Complete Tales*, IV, 498–99)

If there is humor in Miss Sturdy's violent protest against the tyranny of the young, there is also a warning against the indiscriminate glorification of youth. There is whimsy in the Honorable Edward Antrobus' solemn statement that American children are better educated than their elders; but there is also danger implicit in the notion that immaturity is more desirable than maturity. A society that must designate its old people as "senior citizens" in order to avoid the opprobrium associated with aging, needs to examine its values more carefully. James projected this truth in his fiction, at times in the comic mode, often in the ironic, but always with perspicuity and a sense of personal involvement.

"Pandora," which first appeared in the *New York Sun,* June 1 and 8, 1884, (*Complete Tales,* V) is an early example of the novelist's fascination with the alert, young American girl who is able to rise above her environment and realize her potential without the help of her parents. Pandora Day is the first of James's "self-made" girls. Essentially she is a successful Daisy Miller. Like Daisy, she functions without guidance; unlike Daisy, however, Pandora flourishes in spite of parental indifference—indeed it is she who guides her parents. Mr. and Mrs. Day are even more vague than Daisy Miller's indecisive mother. They are "passive and patient" to the point of abdicating completely to their daughter, who, in effect, "runs them." This theme of the child forced through adult neglect to become its own parent is reiterated throughout James's subsequent tales of childhood and adolescence. Pandora is significant because she is the novelist's earliest portrait of the self-reliant young girl who must, of necessity, shape her own destiny.

The story is told from the point of view of Count Otto Vogelstein, an intelligent but humorless secretary of the German legation in Washington. The tale chronicles his several meetings with Pandora Day, "the latest, freshest fruit of our great American evolution . . . the self-made girl!" Count Vogelstein gets his first glimpse of Pandora on board ship on his way to America. The count is "serious, civil, ceremonious, stiff, inquisitive, stuffed with knowledge and convinced that at present the German empire is the country in the world most highly evolved." He is eager to comprehend the oddities of the American scene and quite certain that its vulgarities must be many. He is baffled by Pandora, who is charming, gracious, and beautiful; if she is much too "free" in her deportment, she cannot yet be called vulgar. What is poor Vogelstein to make of it all?

With tongue in cheek, James has him reading "a Tauchnitz novel by an American author whose pages, he had been assured, would help to prepare him" for the strange Americans he was to encounter. Author and title are not given, but before too long we realize that the Count is reading *Daisy Miller*. He identifies Pandora with Daisy. He is, however, surprised to observe before the journey is half over, that he was wrong: "Vogelstein by this time had finished his little American story, and now definitely judged that Pandora Day was not at all like the heroine. She was quite another type; much more serious and preoccupied, and not at all keen, as he had supposed, about making the acquaintance of gentlemen." (*Complete Tales*, V, 368) This is not the last surprise in store for the Count, and James does a credible job of juxtaposing the stuffy young man's Germanic, aristocratic views with American, easy-going attitudes toward class distinction. Vogelstein is conceived in the tradition of the comedy of manners.

Like Daisy Miller, Pandora has a younger brother and James obviously wished to draw a parallel between young Day and Randolph:

> . . . he was only nineteen. If his sister did not resemble the dreadful little girl in the tale I have so often mentioned, there was, for Vogelstein, at least, an analogy between young Mr. Day and a certain small brother—a candy-loving Madison, Hamilton, or Jefferson—who, in the Tauchnitz volume, was attributed to that unfortunate maid. This was what little Madison would have grown up to at nineteen, and the improvement was greater than might have been expected. (*Complete Tales*, V, 369)

Although Pandora's brother is an improvement over Randolph, he is not really socially acceptable to Vogelstein. He may have a face that is "not disagreeable" and be, in his way, "very remarkable" for his age, but James's heart was not in the rehabilitation of Randolph, and it is doubtful whether Vogelstein, the aristocratic snob, would have taken such a view of Pandora's brother.

Pandora captures the imagination of the Count; the observation, identification, and classification of Pandora become the main business of the tale. It would seem that

James—because the question of the American versus the European young girl held great interest for him and because two sides of a "case" always intrigued him—wanted to capture, isolate, and identify those qualities in young American womanhood which were positive and constructive. If American parents were not going to help their children achieve distinction in the American social hierarchy, then a new type must of necessity emerge, a self-sufficient young person who would be "self-made":

> She was possible, doubtless, only in America. . . . She was not fast nor emancipated nor crude nor loud, and there was not in her, of necessity at least, a grain of the stuff of which the adventuress is made. She was simply very successful, and her success was entirely personal. She had not been born with the silver spoon of social opportunity; she had grasped it by honest exertion. You knew her by many different signs, but chiefly, infallibly, by the appearance of her parents . . . you always saw that her parents could never have made her. (*Complete Tales*, V, 397)

But James did not really believe that one could achieve social success by "honest exertion" and without parental guidance. This is why his efforts on behalf of Pandora Day come to naught. James was too firmly committed to the idea that only a society rich in tradition, with long established institutions, could produce a successful person. True success meant cultivation, graciousness, the fruits of an old civilization, and these could hardly be acquired "more or less by reading . . . and conversation garnished with literary allusions, even sudden quotations." In spite of the author's attempts to dissociate himself from Vogelstein's point of view, he shares the Count's half-hearted enthusiasm for the "self-made" girl. Where Daisy Miller is believable and touching, her "successful" counterpart is unconvincing and fails to engage our sympathy.

James's ambivalence toward his heroine—an ambivalence he was to exhibit again and again in his portraits of young girls—diminishes the comic effect the novelist obviously sought in "Pandora Day." The same can be said of "The Chaperon," a later variation on the theme of the reversal of roles in the child-parent relationship. Rose Tramore, the young heroine of the tale, is even more skillful at managing for herself than was Pandora Day. Where Pandora merely creates a place for herself in society without parental assistance, Rose, having secured her own position, successfully rehabilitates her socially ostracized mother as well. "Pandora" and "The Chaperon" do not ring true possibly because they are comic variations on what was, for James, fundamentally a serious theme. Yet the unconvincingly aggressive, "self-made" Pandora, who can even "manage" the President of the United States, is a harbinger of the more substantial and serious young heroines who were to appear in the novels and tales of the late 1890's.

Between 1884 and 1888 James produced five tales specifically concerned with the mother-child relationship. These stories differ in tone and treatment, but essentially they dramatize a precept of conduct that James held which parents were obliged to follow—they must not manipulate their children in order to satisfy their own needs. Whether the impulse to dominate a child hides behind the genteel façade of a Marie Temperly in "Mrs. Temperly," whether it is manifest in the foolish diplomatic maneuvering of Mrs. Daintry of "A New England Summer," or whether it reveals itself in the "expiatory" act of Mrs. Pallant in "Louisa Pallant," meddling in the life of a young adult is an act of gross injustice. It will not, it cannot, accomplish the parent's manifest purpose, and it is usually indicative of parental aggressiveness and hostility toward the child. These mothers as delineated by James are "hard" women. Georgina Gressie, of "Georgina's Reasons," is unbelievably cruel; this "heroine's" need to make her will prevail drives her to commit bigamy and abandon her child to his death. Latent or manifest, presented in the form of social comedy or bitter ironic comment, perversion of what James (in his tribute to his own mother) called the "divine commission" of motherhood is denounced in these tales of maternal manipulation of the young.

"The Patagonia," published in the *English Illustrated Magazine*, August–September, 1888, (*Complete Tales*, VII) is a melancholy little tale on the now-familiar theme of parental laxity. The heroine's insensitive mother pressures her toward a marriage that is intolerable for her. The young woman throws herself into the sea rather than face the "exemplary and very poor" bespectacled young "man of long preparations" who is waiting to marry her in Paris. The children in the tale, the raucous "four little Pecks," offspring of a malicious and vulgar fellow-passenger on *The Patagonia,* are emblematic of the dreary, uncivilized existence Grace Mavis is determined to escape. Mother Peck is too busy informing her fellow-passengers how many years Miss Mavis has been engaged to the gentleman in Paris to notice the behavior of her children: "The four little Pecks, in the enjoyment of untrammelled leisure, swarmed about the ship as if they had been pirates boarding her, and their mother was as powerless to check their license as if she had been gagged and stowed away in the hold. They were especially to be trusted to run between the legs of the stewards when these attendants arrived with bowls of soup for the languid ladies." (*Complete Tales,* VII, 315) These are the children the reader would expect Mrs. Peck to have, and they reinforce our contention that for the novelist, parents are the true culprits.

Parental irresponsibility took many and varied forms in James's fiction, and consequences of it, though invariably destructive, were manifest in diverse ways. In "A London Life," which appeared in *Scribner's Magazine,* June–September, 1888, (*Complete Tales,* VII) the novelist demonstrated yet another species of parental laxity, the consequences of which, though more subtle, are equally disturbing. The major focus of the tale is on the manners and mores of the British aristocracy; the disparity between the gracious decorum of the public life and the chaotic immorality of the private existence is projected through the over-wrought response of an American "innocent" to her sister's marital problems. The children in the tale serve as a gloss on James's social commentary. These "chubby," unfeeling little products of the British landed gentry exemplify a kind of parental neglect that produces insensitive and unresponsive adults.

Laura Wing, the impoverished, puritanical "innocent" from America, is living in material splendour on the estate of her aristocratic English brother-in-law, Lionel Berrington, and his wife, Selina. She is shocked by the relation between husband and wife. It soon becomes clear to Laura that their marriage is a farce, that they are each unfaithful to the other and heading for the divorce courts and scandal, a situation that terrifies the young woman. Laura Wing is exemplary of James's "immature" heroines. Her hysteria over the situation in her sister's home, her inability to accept the reality of evil, and her failure to come to terms with it prefigures the young governess in "The Turn of the Screw." Like her more famous successor, Laura's vision of reality is warped, a condition that, for James, signified stunted intellectual, emotional, and spiritual growth. She is one of his earlier heroines who stands in direct contrast to Maisie Farange of *What Maisie Knew* and Nanda Brookenham of *The Awkward Age,* young people who were able—by virture of their unclouded vision—to achieve emotional and moral completeness. Because Laura is unable to maintain a balanced view of the situation, the disorder, which follows in the wake of the failure of her sister's marriage, overwhelms her.

Two small boys, products of this unhappy union, are relegated to the care of a foolish and sentimental governess, Miss Steet. During the course of the tale, James has some vigorous comments to make on the depravity that lies beneath the surface of London society and the futility of puritanical opposition to it; but more than this, there is the implication of the effect of irresponsibility on the sensibilities of the young. In effect, James is saying that a lack of moral obligation, an absence of ethical standards of behavior in parents reduces children to an animal-like state. He makes this clear through his choice of images and in his subtle rendering of the physical setting. The charm of the scene is contrasted with the dehumanizing process taking place in the children:

[Laura] liked even better the last half-hour in the schoolroom, with the bread and butter, the candles and the red fire, the little spasms of confidence of Miss Steet the nursery-governess, and the society of Scratch and Parson (their nicknames would have made you think they were dogs) her small, magnificent nephews, whose flesh was so firm yet so soft and their eyes so charming when they listened to stories. . . . The place was a setting for rosy childhood, and Laura believed her sister never knew how delightful Scratch and Parson looked there. (*Complete Tales*, VII, 87, 104)

Laura's sister is too busy with dinner parties, theatres, and lovers to take an interest in the affairs of the nursery: "Selina was not without her ideas of decorum—very far from it indeed; only she erected them in such queer places. She was not familiar with . . . the children themselves." (*Complete Tales*, VII, 102) Like his wife, Lionel "was fond of his children, but saw them hardly more frequently than their mother and they never knew whether he were at home or away." Lionel and Selina are completely self-absorbed. James's treatment of the two little boys demonstrates his close observation of children. He knew that youngsters of this age could be counted on to say things that embarrass their elders; what *these* children innocently say defines them, their situation, and their prospects for the future. Ferdy and Geordie are arguing about why their father does not keep hounds as their grandfather did:

"I know—it's because mamma is an American!" Ferdy announced, with confidence.
"And what has that to do with it?" asked Laura.
"Mamma spends so much money—there isn't any more for anything!"
This startling speech elicited an alarmed protest from Miss Steet; she blushed and assured Laura that she couldn't imagine where the child could have picked up such an extraordinary idea. (*Complete Tales*, VII, 107)

James knew that children absorb, as if by osmosis, the feelings, attitudes, and prejudices of their elders. In spite of admonitions by Miss Steet and Laura, Geordie has had his impression. " 'I shan't get married—I want to have hounds,' proclaimed Geordie, who had apparently been much struck with his brother's explanation."

The animal references could hardly have been accidental. Geordie and Ferdy have nicknames that remind Laura of dogs and they prefer hounds to people. The children reveal themselves and their milieu with every sentiment they express. When Miss Steet suggests to Laura that they have some music together after dinner, Geordie says, "Oh music—we don't go in for music." And he says it "with clear superiority." When Lionel, under the influence of alcohol, makes one of his rare appearances in the nursery, "the little boys asked him no questions to celebrate his return" nor are they interested in the fact that their mother has gone off and left them. They have learned that disinterest is a refuge when dealing with unpredictable adults. Lionel creates an unpleasant scene when he is about to tell Laura that her sister is in Paris with a lover. The governess, sensing their father's irresponsibility, "gathered Geordie and Ferdy together and swept them out of the room." It becomes obvious where the children pick up their "extraordinary ideas" and why they have already developed a protective impassivity in response to adults. The price these children will pay for living comfortably with themselves will be the shutting off of emotion and thought; the tragedy of their plight will never be perceived by them or by those with whom they come in contact; they will simply never know what it is like to feel deeply about anything. They will not even be capable of eliciting pity. Laura makes this observation:

> The children stood on either side of her, leaning against her, and she had an arm round each; their little bodies were thick and strong and their voices had the quality of silver bells. Their mother had certainly gone too far; but there was nevertheless a limit to the tenderness one could feel for the neglected, compromised bairns. It was difficult to take a sentimental view of them—they would never take such a view of themselves. Geordie would grow up to be a master-hand at polo and care more for that pastime than for anything in life, and Ferdy perhaps would develop into "the best shot in England." Laura felt these possibilities stirring within them; they were in the things they said to her, in the things they said to each other. At any rate they would never reflect upon anything in the world. (*Complete Tales*, VII, 106)

Geordie and Ferdy are fashioned by the same incongruities and duplicities as are their parents. Their lives would inevitably be dedicated to the perpetuation of a surface decorum that would hide contention and corruption beneath a veneer of manners; their defense against the tedium of such an existence, the "blessed" faculty for cut-

ting themselves off from deeply felt experience. Through
Geordie and Ferdy Berrington, James has given us a recognizable portrait of one segment of the British aristocracy;
he has demonstrated, as well, his commitment to the idea
of parental duty as inseparable from social responsibility.

During two decades—from 1870 to 1890—concepts and
feelings about children and their parents took on a certain
concreteness for James; the result was the formulation of
a tangible theory of education that we see reflected in his
subsequent fictional representations of childhood and adolescence. One of the novelist's most explicit fictional statements on the education of the young is found in "Greville
Fane," which appeared in the *Illustrated London News* on
September 17 and 24, 1892. (*Complete Tales*, VIII) By this
time James's theory of education was based on the proposition that maximum awareness is indispensable for maximum growth. Blind, deluded parents could not hope to
raise children with vision necessary to see them through
to maturity; neither could they entertain unrealistic hopes
nor set unattainable goals for their offspring. The attitudes expressed in fictional form in "Greville Fane" were
not new; James had been thinking about these problems
for many years. He recorded the basic idea for the tale in
his notebook on January 22, 1879. In this entry he conjectures about a theory—attributed to Anthony Trollope and
reiterated by Miss Thackeray—that a child might "be
brought up to be a novelist as to any other trade." [5] The
development of the artist was, in James's fiction, often to
parallel the development of the human being, and the
absurdity of the notion that an artist could be fashioned
at will, without regard for his natural endowment, suggested that "one might make a little story upon this." At
the time (in 1879) he saw it as "a comment—a satire—
upon high parental views." By 1892, however, the nurture
of an artist required more than natural endowment; it required proper parental example. In its final form the tale
becomes an uncompromising statement on yet another
kind of "spoiled" child—one who is the victim of its

5. *The Notebooks of Henry James*, ed. F. O. Matthiessen and
Kenneth B. Murdock (New York, 1962), p. 10.

parent's self-delusion and degraded values. From the first
James saw the parent as "a literary lady (a poor novelist)"
and the child's education as "peculiar." In a subsequent
notebook entry—February 27, 1889—he elaborated on the
original idea but this time with a shift in emphasis to the
educational theory behind the notion of bringing up a
child "to write novels as a lucrative trade."

Mrs. Stormer (who writes superficial, artistically worthless but highly popular novels under the pen-name of
Greville Fane) decides that since the life of a popular
novelist is pleasant and lucrative, she will educate her son
to be a writer like herself. The artistic imperfections of
the deluded lady-novelist become emblematic of her deficiencies as a mother. She is presented from the ironic, yet
not unsympathetic, point of view of the narrator, an intelligent, sensitive, and (unlike Greville Fane) a gifted
writer:

> Greville Fane's ignorance of life was a resource still more un-
> failing than the most approved receipt. . . . "With me it's
> different; I try, in my clumsy way, to be in some direct rela-
> tion to life." "Oh, bother your direct relation to life!" she used
> to reply, for she was always annoyed by the phrase. . . .
> (*Complete Tales*, VIII, 438, 439)

The deluded mother sees her son through a mist of un-
reality just as the misguided novelist sees her fictional
characters through a mist of sentimentality. The "system"
she had devised for her son's education bore the same
relationship to the actual world as the adulterous duch-
esses and mustachioed guardsmen who peopled her fiction: "He grew up in gorgeous apparel, which was his way
of interpreting his mother's system. Whenever I met her
I found her still under the impression that she was carrying this system out and that Leolin's training was bearing
fruit. She was giving him experience, she was giving him
impressions, she was putting a *gagne-pain* into his hand.
It was another name for spoiling him with the best conscience in the world." (*Complete Tales*, VIII, 442)

Mrs. Stormer's project is doomed to fail, of course, and
Leolin becomes a ne'er-do-well. James is careful to tell us,
through the narrator, exactly why: "His mother's theory

of the happy knack he could pick up deprived him of the wholesome discipline required to prevent young idlers from becoming cads. He had, abroad, a casual tutor and a snatch or two of a Swiss school, but no consecutive study, no prospect of a university or a degree. It may be imagined with what zeal, as the years went on, he entered into the pleasantry of there being no manual so important to him as the massive book of life." (*Complete Tales*, VIII, 444-45)

In spite of Greville Fane's failure to perceive reality, her misguided educational theory, and her blind, distorted love for her son, she engages our sympathy. James has captured the pathos of her foolish delusion: "She loved the young imposter with a simple, blind, benighted love, and of all the heroes of romance who passed before her eyes he was by far the most brilliant. He was at any rate the most real—she could touch him, pay for him, suffer for him, worship him. He made her think of her princes and dukes, and when she wished to fix these figures in her mind's eye she thought of her boy." (*Complete Tales*, VIII, 447)

Greville Fane made the mistake—fatal to success as a parent and destructive of artistic creativity—of assuming she could experience life vicariously: "She held, not unjustly, that the sincere novelist should feel the whole flood of life; she acknowledged with regret that she had not time to feel it herself, and it was a joy to her that the deficiency might be supplied by the sight of the way it was rushing through this magnificent young man." (*Complete Tales*, VIII, 447)

It is clear that James was concerned with more than conditions of growth for the creative artist for he introduces Greville Fane's daughter into the tale. Ethel Stormer's education was no less carefully planned than that of her brother, despite the fact that Mrs. Stormer did not intend to make a novelist of her: "She devoted much thought and many thousands of francs to the education of her daughter, who spent three years at a very superior school at Dresden, receiving wonderful instruction in sciences, arts and tongues, and who, taking a different line from Leolin, was to be brought up wholly as a *femme du monde*. (*Complete Tales*, VIII, 443)

While Ethel was given the formal instruction that Leolin, in the interest of cultivating his "creativity," was denied, she was never, either by precept or example, taught the basic decencies of human relations. Because Greville Fane is essentially nothing more than a "clever and vulgar and snobbish" woman, her daughter is given the wrong set of values by which to live. The lack of discrimination reflected in the mother's novels, where "the immoral and the maternal lived together . . . on the most comfortable terms," was inevitably a decisive factor in the formation of her daughter's character. Ethel grows up to be "cold and affected and ambitious"—the embodiment of the heartlessness implicit in her mother's snobbery. The girl makes a "brilliant" marriage to Sir Baldwin Luard, an impoverished aristocrat whom Mrs. Stormer must help out financially from time to time. And in spite of the fact "that of all [Greville Fane's] productions 'my daughter Lady Luard' was quite the one she was proudest of . . . that personage thought her mother vulgar and was distressed and perplexed by the occasional license of her pen. . . ." Mrs. Stormer is not welcome at her daughter's home because Ethel "doesn't want her friends to ask if [her mother has ever] known nice people."

Because "correctness was the virtue in the world that, like her heroes and heroines, she valued least," Greville Fane was an inferior novelist and a destructive mother. Her children, like her novels, were "spoiled" by delusion and amorality. At the end of the tale James emphasizes the association between distortion in art and perversion of the mission of parenthood. Having never succeeded in writing anything on his own, Leolin is paid by his mother to give her "ideas" for her own novels:

. . . in addition to his salary he was paid by the piece: he got so much for a striking character, so much for a pretty name, so much for a plot, so much for an incident, and had so much promised him if he would invent a new crime.
"He *has* invented one," I said, "and he's paid every day of his life." (*Complete Tales*, VIII, 451)

Mrs. Stormer does not appear to understand that the crime Leolin invented (and which she helped him perpetrate) was that of his own destruction through his exploitation of her weakness:

> "What is it?" she asked, looking hard at the picture of the year, "Baby's Tub," near which we happened to be standing.
> I hesitated a moment. "I myself will write a little story about it, and then you'll see."
> But she never saw; she had never seen anything and she passed away with her fine blindness unimpaired. (*Complete Tales*, VIII, 451–52)

In characteristic fashion, James leaves the reader wondering if the poor woman did not in fact see a glimmer of the truth in "the picture of the year" at which she looked so hard. If she did, the vision of reality came too late; the damage was beyond repair. At the root of Greville Fane's terrible defeat was an unforgivable failure of perception; without vision the creation of art and the education of the young are impossible. This Jamesian principle of education is implicit in the notebook entry of 1879, and it is fully stated in the tale of 1892. It had been axiomatic for James from the first that indifferent, selfish, or unloving parents could not raise loving children. It became increasingly clear to him as well, that vulgar, deluded parents could not hope to produce cultivated and sensitive offspring. Although he had implied in "Pandora" that heightened sensibility in the young could triumph over the baser aspects of human nature, it was not until later in his career that James would dramatize the situation effectively.

In these tales dealing with child-parent relations, James speaks out clearly and resolutely in placing the blame for the "spoiled" child where it belongs. The fact that most critics have, by and large, ignored this aspect of his thought is to be deplored, and it is puzzling that others have found his more concentrated preoccupation with these problems in the 1890's to be "morbid." Dorothea Krook is one of the few who recognized James's true intent:

> I believe that James was moved to a compassion (and a horror) beyond the imagination of his critics by the sufferings of

the helpless young in the society which he came to know so intimately. The injuries, psychological and moral, that irresponsible, self-centered, pleasure-seeking parents of the leisured class could inflict upon their children by simple neglect . . . or by positive exploitation . . . or by still subtler forms of violation . . . was—and still is—a matter of daily observation in the life of this society; and James's concern with these phenomena, so far from being unhealthy and morbid, shows rather the healthiest moral revulsion from these unlovely aspects of the upper-class society of his day.[6]

Mrs. Krook is referring specifically to the Jamesian children of the 1890's, but what she says of the impulse that lay behind James's creation of them is equally true of his earlier children. Maisie, Morgan, and Nanda did not suddenly materialize out of thin air for their creator. They are the logical successors to Master Eustace, Randolph Miller, Geordie Berrington, and Leolin Stormer. Unique in his fictional rendering of the "spoiled" child is the intensity of James's anger at the "spoilers," an anger that he felt early in his career, never ceased to feel, and one that was to become subsumed in the artist when, in his maturity, he produced some of the most memorable children in English and American literature.

6. Dorothea Krook, *The Ordeal of Consciousness in Henry James* (Cambridge, England, 1962), p. 114.

CHAPTER IV

Determinism
and "Sacrificed" Children

Henry James retained his vision of the victimized child in every phase of his development as an artist. His method of presentation and his emphasis shifted, however, at different stages in his career. In his early and more primitive tales of the 1860's, we have noted that children are presented as victims of invisable, unknown forces; no relationship of cause and effect exists between what they do and what is done to them. As James's art matured, his treatment of this theme became more complex. In his middle period, during the 1880's, heredity and environment are causal factors in the ultimate fate of some of his fictional children. The destructive force in these instances is no longer some undefined, vindictive power. What the child is, and what he is subjected to, determine his destiny. The children of his third and mature phase are decisively affected by their immediate environment. They often become instruments of their elders' hostilities and aggressions, tools adults use to destroy each other; without exception they are victims of a morally deficient adult world.

James assumes, throughout his fiction, that the source of value in life is to be found in the quality of relationships between human beings. People must not "use" people for their own ends. The children of the middle period are the creations of a novelist who was also actively concerned with social problems of his time.

On Christmas Eve of 1878, James accompanied a lady of his acquaintance on an errand of charity. His friend was going to an English workhouse to distribute gifts to unfortunate children confined there, and James, ever eager for new impressions, went with her. His record of the experience, incorporated in an essay which appeared in *The Nation* in 1879, suggests his awareness of the broader social and economic environment which directly influences the child:

I have said that the place reminded me of "Oliver Twist," and I glanced through this little herd for an infant figure that should look as if it were cut out for romantic adventure. But they were all very prosaic little mortals. They were made of very common clay indeed, and a certain number of them were idiotic. They filed up and received their little offerings, and then compressed themselves into a tight infantine bunch, and lifting up their small hoarse voices, directed a melancholy hymn toward their benefactress. The scene was a picture I shall not forget, with its curious mixture of poetry and sordid prose—the dying wintry light in the big, bare, stale room; the beautiful Lady Bountiful, standing in the twinkling glory of the christmas tree; the little multitude of staring and wondering, yet perfectly expressionless faces.[1]

The detached reportorial stance, the objective tone, the documentary quality of the diction suggest that as early as 1879, James shared the interest of his French, English, and American contemporaries in the effect of environment on the life of the child. At this time, James tended to deal with childhood in retrospect in his fiction. We meet his characters as adults already formed and deeply engaged in the business of coming to terms with life. Ever aware of the impact of "conditioning" on the life of the individual, James permits the reader a glimpse of determining factors. By dramatizing crucial moments in the childhood of his characters, the novelist suggests the multiplicity of relations that formed them.

This is particularly evident in *The Bostonians* and *The Princess Casamassima*, both published in 1886. In this excursion into the world of the naturalistic novel—that is, the determinist novel—James documented the "learning theory" to which certain of his characters had been subjected. In part, he was responding to the currents of scientific and philosophical thought that dominated the

1. Henry James, "The New Year in England," *The Nation*, XXIII (January, 23, 1879), 65.

decade and profoundly altered the form and content of fiction of the period. The impact of Darwin on imaginative literature of the day was considerable, and James's novels of this decade show a predisposition he shared with French naturalists, notably with Emil Zola, whom he read attentively.

While *The Bostonians*[2] is, in some respects, unique in the James canon, it is thoroughly consistent with attitudes expressed in works of his middle and late phases. I refer specifically to his conviction that the child is a product of his environment; it determines the kind of adult he will be, a psychological truth the novelist had come to recognize as early as 1870. The heroine of *The Bostonians*, Verena Tarrant, possesses a "mystical faculty," a strange eloquence, the source of which is documented in detail:

> She had been nursed in darkened rooms, and suckled in the midst of manifestations, she had begun to "attend lectures," as she said, when she was quite an infant, because her mother had no one to leave her with at home. She sat on the knees of somnambulists, and had been passed from hand to hand by trance-speakers; she was familiar with every kind of "cure," and had grown up among lady-editors of newspapers advocating new religions, and people who disapproved of the marriage-tie. Verena talked of the marriage-tie as she would have talked of the last novel—as if she heard it as frequently discussed. (*Bostonians*, pp. 84–85)

With this economical recreation of Verena's childhood, the author sets the tone and makes clear the attitude the reader may take toward the girl's "gift" of eloquence. James is not content, however, with the obvious apposition of cause and effect. He probes deeply into the emotional tie between the girl and her father.

Dr. Tarrant is described as having mesmeric power over his daughter. She can speak only when she is under his spell. "Well, I can't say much except when father has worked on me," she tells Olive Chancellor. "He is very good," Verena said simply. "And he's wonderfully magnetic." The girl's attachment to her father is an odd one and lends itself to interpretation on a level other than the obvious. It accounts, I believe, for Verena's "pure femi-

2. Henry James, *The Bostonians* (New York, 1956).

nine center," which makes it possible for her to form a normal, if not necessarily happy, union with Basil Ransom. The love that she feels for her father, the faith that she has in him makes it easy for her to transfer these feelings to another male. Without these feelings and the social situation that permitted them free expression, Verena's capitulation to Ransom might have seemed less credible. As James created her, she is excessively malleable, and Olive Chancellor, with her pathological need to possess the girl, is a formidable contender for Verena's affection and loyalty. The peculiar nature of the girl's kinship with her father is vividly presented in the scene when Verena speaks for the first time at the meeting in Miss Birdseye's home:

. . . Verena . . . raised her eyes . . . silently now, with the same sweetness, and then rested them on her father. This gentleman seemed to respond to an irresistible appeal; he looked round at the company with all his teeth, and said that these flattering allusions were not so embarrassing as they might otherwise be, inasmuch as any success that he and his daughter might have had was so thoroughly impersonal: he insisted on that word. They had just heard her say, "It is not *me*, mother," and he and Mrs. Tarrant and the girl herself were equally aware it was not she. It was some power outside—it seemed to flow through her. . . . When he just calmed her down by laying his hand on her a few moments, it seemed to come . . . in the West it had taken the form of a considerable eloquence. (*Bostonians*, pp. 55–56)

The dramatic action that follows Dr. Tarrant's explanation and precedes Verena's performance reinforces the reader's impression of the singular bond between father and daughter. The girl gets up and goes to the doctor who is standing in the center of the room:

Verena took her father's hands, held them for a moment, while she stood before him, not looking at him, with eyes toward the company; then, after an instant, her mother, rising, pushed forward, with an interesting sigh, the chair on which she had been sitting. Mrs. Tarrant was provided with another seat, and Verena, relinquishing her father's grasp, placed herself in the chair, which Tarrant put in position for her. She sat there with closed eyes, and her father now rested his long, lean hands upon her head . . . she was very quiet now . . . and her father continued the mysterious process of calming her down. . . . Dr. Tarrant looked at no one as he stroked and soothed his daughter. . . . "Quietly—quietly," he murmured, from time to time, "It will come, my good child, it will come. Just let it work—just let it gather. The spirit, you know; you've got to let the spirit come out when it will." (*Bostonians*, pp. 58–60)

Mrs. Tarrant surrenders her seat with an "interesting sigh" to her daughter who becomes articulate when she has taken her mother's place and entered into a communion with her father that excludes the outside world. Basil Ransom reacts with understandable irritation to the little drama being enacted before him. He grows impatient of Dr. Tarrant's "grotesque manipulations, which he resented as much as if he himself felt their touch, and which seemed a dishonor to the passive maiden. They made him nervous, they made him angry." Ransom, possessive and jealous, is angered and repelled by the depth of feeling he senses between Verena and her father. James's rendering of Verena's total personality (that aspect which has its roots in "conditioning" and that which is unique in its response to the father) breathes life into what might otherwise have been the portrait of a foolish and hysterical young woman.

In *The Princess Casamassima*, the second of James's naturalistic novels, young Hyacinth Robinson is perhaps the most Dickensian of his fictional children. In true Jamesian fashion, however, his waif would have to be "some individual sensitive nature or fine mind, some small obscure intelligent creature whose education should have been almost wholly derived from [the London streets] capable of profiting by all the civilization, all the accumulations to which they testify, yet condemned to see these things only from outside—in mere quickened consideration, mere wistfulness and envy and despair." [3] Hyacinth is for all the world one of those "prosaic little mortals" who impressed James on his visit to the workhouse in 1878; the novelist's imagination has supplied the necessary ingredients for the "romantic adventure." In short, he took what was fundamentally a Dickensian

3. Henry James, *The Art of the Novel*, ed. R. P. Blackmur (New York, 1934), p. 60.

child and endowed him with a Jamesian sensibility. Hyacinth's commitment to the anarchist cause had to be rooted in more than resentment at a society that withheld its benefits from the deprived and brutalized masses. In his preface to *The Princess*, James leaves not doubt of his intention: "[Hyacinth's] being jealous of all the ease of life of which he tastes so little, and, bitten, under this exasperation, with an aggressive, vindictive, destructive social faith, his turning to 'treason, stratagems and spoils' might be as vivid a picture as one chose, but would move to pity and terror only by the aid of some deeper complication, some imposed and formidable issue." [4] Hyacinth's thirst for the beauty and civilization of a world he is pledged to destroy is the "deeper complication" that gives the novel its ironic dimension and moves the reader to sympathy for the dispossessed child.

In his illuminating introduction to the 1948 edition of *The Princess Casamassima*, Lionel Trilling relates Hyacinth's aesthetic hunger to his deprivation, in early youth, of parental love; he feels that Hyacinth never matured, that indeed he dies emotionally still a child because of the "withdrawal of love." "The intention is not to show him as unmanly but as too young to make the claims of maturity; he is the child of the book. . . . And this child-man lives in a novel full of parental figures. Hyacinth has no less than three sets of parents . . . the decisive parental pair are, of course, the actual parents, Lord Frederick and Florentine, who represent . . . the forces which are in conflict in Hyacinth." [5]

The child's conflict is dramatically presented at the beginning of the novel in the chapter dealing with Hyacinth's journey to prison to meet his dying mother. In order to achieve authenticity in his rendering of the setting, James determined to experience it first hand. In a letter to Thomas Sargeant Perry in 1884, he wrote, "I have been all the morning at Millbank Prison (horrible place) collecting notes for a fiction scene. You see I am

4. Ibid., p. 72.
5. Lionel Trilling in his Introduction to Henry James, *The Princess Casamassima* (New York, 1948), pp. xxvi-xxvii.

quite the Naturalist. Look out for same—a year hence." [6]
The eventual product of James's visit is indeed memorable. He captured the misery, despair, and violence to human dignity which characterizes prison life. But for all
the obvious attempt at a naturalistic depiction of the
child in the tradition of David Copperfield or Oliver Twist,
the chapter remains notable for its unusual insight into
how a small child thinks, feels, and acts. The focus is on
the sensitive little boy's response to every aspect of a
situation he does not understand and will not fully assimilate until much later in life. The child is curious, like
most children, and eager for adventure; in this mood he
starts out on the trip to the prison. We sense Hyacinth's
vulnerability through Miss Pysent's perception of the situation: "It seemed to her an adventure as dangerous as
it was dismal, and she was immensely touched by the
clearfaced eagerness of the child at her side, who strained
forward as brightly as he had done on another occasion
. . . when she had taken him to the tower. (*Princess
Casamassima*, p. 36)

The boy is not told the true purpose of the trip to the
jail, but children interpret with astonishing accuracy
what adults say and how they really feel about what they
are saying. Hyacinth "wanted to know everything about
everything and he projected the fierce light of his questions on Miss Pysent's incarcerated friend." The child
"listened to her history with absorbed attention and then
said: 'And hadn't she any children—hadn't she a little
boy?'" The child has a vague presentiment of his true relationship to the woman in prison. Miss Pysent's anxiety
has communicated itself to him. He senses her awe at
the "big dark-towered building . . . lying there and
sprawling over the whole neighborhood with brown,
bare, windowless walls, ugly truncated pinnacles and a
character unspeakably sad and stern." If it evoked "a
dreadful premonitory sinking of the heart" in Miss Pysent, it did as much for Hyacinth:

6. Virginia Harlow, *Thomas Sergeant Perry: A Biography* (Durham, North Carolina, 1950), p. 319.

The child suddenly jerked away his hand and, placing it behind him in the clutch of the other, said to her respectfully but resolutely, while he planted himself at a considerable distance:

"I don't like this place."

"Neither do I like it, my darling," cried the dressmaker, pitifully. "Oh, if you knew how little!"

"Then we'll go away. I won't go in." (*Princess Casamassima*, pp. 38–39)

Miss Pysent's talk of "expiation" and "goodness" achieved through suffering strengthens the child's apprehension that his fate is inextricably bound up with that of the incarcerated woman. This sense of affinity impels him to enter the dingy, forbidding prison:

He transferred his remarkable little eyes—eyes which always appeared to her to belong to a person older and stronger than herself—to her face; and then he put to her: "Why should I save such a creature if I don't like her?"

"If she likes you, that will be enough."

At this Miss Pysent began to see that he was moved. "Will she like me very much?"

"More, much more, than anyone—ever."

"More than you, now?"

"Oh," said Amanda quickly, "I mean more than she likes anyone." (*Princess Casamassima*, p. 40)

The woman is, in effect, telling the child that he is about to meet his parent. On a subjective level, Hyacinth's hunger for the love of his real mother makes him decide to risk the confrontation, to accept his dubious heritage with all its limitations. " 'Oh well,' he said at last, 'I'll just step in.' " When Miss Pysent tells him that the woman in prison had a baby named Hyacinth, the boy already knows who he is: "Hyacinth's little white face exhibited no confusion; he only turned it to the prisoner again, and Miss Pysent felt that some extraordinary dumb exchange of meaning was taking place between them." (*Princess Casamassima*, pp. 47–48)

But the wasted, dazed creature he sees before him is not a motherly vision. He makes one last desperate attempt to dissociate himself from her:

"Who is that woman? What does she want?" Hyacinth broke out again, his small, clear voice ringing over the dreary room.

"She wants you to come near her, she wants to kiss you,

sir," said [the prison matron], as if it were more than he deserved.

"I won't kiss her; Pinnie says she stole a watch!" the child answered with resolution. (*Princess Casamassima*, p. 48)

When Hyacinth sees the consternation his words have caused Miss Pysent and the dying woman, he regrets his outburst; his devotion to Pinnie as well as his curiosity impel him to approach the bed. What follows is a scene of extraordinary poignancy:

> "I'm very sorry I made you cry. And you must pardon Pinnie—I asked her so many questions."
> These words came from close beside the prostrate dressmaker, who, lifting herself quickly, found the little boy had advanced to her elbow and was taking a nearer view of the mysterious captive. . . . [Florentine] found strength partly to raise herself in her bed again and to hold out her arms to him with the same thrilling sobs. . . . Amanda caught the child with an eagerness almost as great as Florentine's and, drawing him to the head of the bed, pushed him into his mother's arms. "Kiss her—kiss her well, and we'll go home!" she whispered desperately while they closed about him and the poor dishonored head pressed itself against his young cheek. It was a terrible, irresistible embrace, to which Hyacinth submitted with instant patience . . . there was a minute's stillness during which the boy accommodated himself as he might to his strange ordeal. (*Princess Casamassima*, pp. 49–50)

We are not told the child's thoughts; we see what he does and hear what he says. In this manner James conveys the boy's bewildering experience. The drama unfolds on two levels. On one we are observing a sensitive little boy forced to live through a shocking encounter; on the other there is the quest of the dispossessed for identity. The boy says nothing in the cab on the way home from the prison; he sits "looking out of the window in silence till they re-enter Lomax Place." But the reader knows that the impressions of that day have sunk deeply into the heart and mind of the child. The course of Hyacinth's life will be profoundly affected by them.

James was successful in his retrospective evocation of Hyacinth's childhood experience because he was not content with a merely naturalistic rendering of the episode. We are given the boy in conflict with his heredity, his environment, and himself. This treatment of the small child as a complex, self-doubting entity lifts the episode out of the realm of nineteenth-century naturalism and into the main current of twentieth-century psychological realism.

James followed the lead of many of his contemporaries in the 1880's by giving his theme of the victimized child a naturalistic cast; yet he struck an individual note in his handling of this motif. We can, at this time, observe a parallel development. James's children have evolved, in varying degrees, into instruments of adult hate and revenge, and in certain tales James explores in depth, through the child, various possibilities inherent in human motivation.

One of the earliest examples of James's use of the child as instrument of adult hostility can be found in "The Author of Beltraffio" (1884). (*Complete Tales*, V) In this tale the author examined the possible masks that hate and aggression can assume; he chose a child to embody those qualities most easily destroyed by wrath.

Mrs. Ambient uses her child to humiliate her husband whose liberated imagination and capacity for feeling evoke both terror and envy in her. Nothing less than the death of their child will suffice to punish her husband, who is the embodiment of the sensuality she fears. Less overt is Mark Ambient's anger toward his wife, but it is nonetheless present in the strange satisfaction he seems to derive from the battle of wills taking place between them for possession of the child. He uses his little son to taunt his wife, to exacerbate her anxiety. " 'Dolcino, come see your daddy!' There was something in the way he stood still and waited that made me think he did it for a purpose," the narrator tells us. Ambient's passive resistance to his wife's fierce possessiveness, his way of saying " 'My Dear,' very genially, without a trace of resentment at her detention of the child," gives the reader the feeling that he has his own use to make of little Dolcino, that he, too, is guilty of sacrificing the child on the altar of his egotism.

Miss Ambient, Mark's sister, has a personal score to settle with life, and she does not shrink from giving vent to her frustration through the child. Essentially a lonely, colorless woman, she strains under the burden of anonymity; "Her affectation rubbed off on her brother's renown . . . he was the original, and she was the inevitable imitation." She sees what is going to happen to the child with a "terrible lucidity," yet she does not lift a finger to save Dolcino. What better revenge on a brother whose brilliance robbed her of her identity than to see his most beautiful and meaningful creation destroyed?

The novelist's most subtle rendering of unconscious motivation is embodied in his presentation of the narrator. At first glance an objective and unwilling witness to the terrible events of that weekend, it soon becomes evident that the narrator is not as uninvolved as he believes himself to be. The inescapable fact is that his action leads directly to the tragic death of the little boy, that he is dimly aware of the possible consequences of his meddling, and that he cannot explain his own behavior. While there is no evidence in the story that the narrator is consciously seeking Dolcino's death, or that he is, indeed, more than a young, meddlesome hero-worshiper, there *are* indications in the text that he is unconsciously envious of Ambient. Moments before he gives the child's mother the manuscript that will supply her with the motive for Dolcino's destruction, we are party to his thoughts:

I betook myself to Ambient's study, delighted to have a quiet hour to look over his books by myself. The windows were open into the garden, the sunny stillness, the mild light of the English summer, filled the room, without quite chasing away the rich, dusky air which was part of its charm, and which abode in the serried shelves where old morocco exhaled the fragrance of curious learning, and in the brighter intervals where medals and prints and miniatures were suspended upon a surface of faded stuff. The place had both colour and quiet; I thought it a perfect room for work, and went so far as to say to myself that if it were mine, to sit and scribble in, there was no knowing but that I might learn to write as well as the author of *Beltraffio*. (*Complete Tales*, V, 345–46)

Hero-worship can, on occasion, hide less acceptable feelings, and thoughtless meddling in other people's affairs can sometimes be a way of coping with such feelings. The narrator tells us that Mrs. Ambient's obvious displeasure at his staying on "ought, doubtless, to have made me more careful as to what I said next; but all I can say is that it didn't." And again, "I bade her goodnight, and then, without intention, by a kind of fatality, the perversity of which had already made me insist unduly on talking with her about her husband's achievements, I alluded to the precious proof-sheets. . . ." Exploiting the irony of the situation to its fullest, James has the child supply the rationale for the narrator's final thoughtless interference that leads directly to little Dolcino's death:

The boy's little fixed white face seemed, as before, to plead with me to stay, and after a while it produced still another effect, a very curious one, which I shall find it difficult to express. Of course I expose myself to the charge of attempting to give fantastic reasons for an act which may have been simply the fruit of a native want of discretion; and indeed the traceable consequences of that perversity were too lamentable to leave me any desire to trifle with the question. All I can say is that I acted in perfect good faith, and that Dolcino's friendly little gaze gradually kindled the spark of my inspiration . . . the plea that I speak of, which issued from the child's eyes . . . seemed to make him say, "The mother that bore me and that presses me here to her bosom—sympathetic little organism that I am—has really the kind of sensibility which she has been represented to you as lacking; if you only look for it patiently and respectfully." (*Complete Tales*, V. 343)

Only unconscious jealousy can account for the narrator's failure—in the face of all he has been told and all he witnesses—to perceive the Medea-like fanaticism in Mrs. Ambient. He is sensitive enough to appreciate Ambient's subtle and sophisticated novels; yet in relation to the woman he becomes naïve to the point of simple-mindedness. It seems clear that the narrator is attributing feelings and ideas to the child which will justify his placing the manuscript into the hands of its mother, the proof she needs to convince herself that Dolcino is better off dead than subject to the "corrupting" influence of his father. It is my contention that in this tale James explores the inextricable manner in which contradictory feelings are often comingled in one individual. Love and hate, the forces behind all human behavior, have been woven into the fabric of this tale. Dolcino Ambient is emblematic of beauty, purity, and innocence, qualities James associates with artistic creation. The little boy is placed in a vortex of forces that are antiethical to the survival of art and love, indeed to life itself. For James these forces are egotism, hate, envy, and intolerance; these eventually destroy the child and, by extension, the creative capability of the artist. Dolcino is "used" by the four major adults in the story to give expression to their manifest as well as their latent feelings. In the real world children are too often manipulated by adults seeking to destroy one another, and this invariably is done in the name of some higher ideal connected with the welfare of the child. There seems to be something irresistible about the purity and innocence of childhood, as though the adult must eradicate any vestige of what he no longer possesses. James has created a fictional world in which he exposes the inner mechanism of this human frailty. Little Dolcino is a kind of kaleidoscope through which continually changing forms of hate are viewed, a passive reflector of (and sacrifice to) man's destructive impulse.

The passivity that characterized the victimized children of the 1880's is not in evidence in those of the following decade. In the 90's James's fictional children are conspicuous for their energetic response to experience. A distinctive group of eager, curious, and remarkably active little girls loom large in the stories of the last half of the decade; we meet them in infancy and follow their development from tale to tale as they emerge from childhood into adolescence. Between 1895 and 1900 James seems to be following the evolution of the female child from cradle to adulthood. Beginning with the birth of Effie Bream in *The Other House* (1896), we have, in quick succession, the wise five-year-old Maisie of *What Maisie Knew* (1897) and the vivacious eight-year-old Flora in "The Turn of the Screw" (1898). With Flora, James moves also into adolescence with his characterization of the governess in the same story, the little telegraphist of *In the Cage* (1898), and Nanda Brookenham of *The Awkward Age* (1899). By the end of the decade, the novelist's curious little girls have evolved into mature, fully developed young women. Little boys, in James's fictional world, are less fortunate; they are ruthlessly sacrificed on the altar of adult egotism.[7] The persistence of this pattern in the author's fiction leads inevitably to biography that, although not strictly within the province of the literary critic, raises some interesting questions perhaps relevant to our understanding of the novelist's product. In his biography of James, Leon Edel remarks: "Before the little boy's [James's] observant eyes there was this ever-present picture of ambiguity and reversal of relation: a father strong, robust, manly, yet weak and feminine, soft and yielding, indulging his children at every turn; and a mother strong, firm, but irrational and contradictory."[8]

More than admiration for her strength colored James's feeling for his mother. In his autobiography he speaks of her in the following terms: ". . . what really could exceed the tenderness of our fastening on her that she *was* he [their father], *was* each of us, was our pride and our humility, our possibility of *any* relation, and the very canvas itself on which we were floridly embroidered?"[9]

In contrast to this clear and positive delineation of his mother is his ambivalent portrait of his father which Professor Edel has noted: "Behind the warm show of tenderness and affection, reflecting his conscious feelings towards the senior Henry, we catch his uncertainty and emotional confusion. Every now and again the father peeps from behind his son's flowing sentences as a rather ineffectual old man."[10] Professor Edel's observation is substantiated by James's own remarks; the following passage is but one of many examples to be found in his autobiography:

Detached as I could during all those years . . . believe myself, it would still have done my young mind . . . violence to have

7. For this observation I am indebted to Professor Leon Edel.
8. Leon Edel, *Henry James*, Vol. I, *The Untried Years: 1843–1870* (New York, 1953), pp. 50–51.
9. Henry James, *Notes of a Son and Brother* (New York, 1914), pp. 179–80.
10. Edel, *The Untried Years*, p. 51.

to suppose that any plane of conclusion for him [his father] . . . could be in the nature of a fool's paradise. Small vague outsider as I was, I couldn't have borne *that* possibility; and I see . . . how little I really could ever have feared it. This would have amounted to fearing it on account of his geniality —a shocking supposition; as if his geniality had been thin and *bête*, patched up and poor, and not . . . of the very stuff of his genius. . . .[11]

James's adult fictional heroes attest his association of weakness with masculinity as his full-grown heroines reflect his correlation of strength with femininity. One wonders, however, whether this ambiguous reversal of roles, which undoubtedly existed between the novelist's parents, tells the whole story of the ruthlessly sacrificed male children. Without insisting too much on what might conceivably have gone on in James's psyche, one can, perhaps, question whether the author's propensity for killing off little boys implies a feeling of guilt in relation to maleness. Could not James's strong identification with his mother have awakened feelings that, like his fictional creation, Master Eustace, he found impossible to acknowledge, feelings of guilt, complicated by his attitude toward his father, which could only be assuaged by symbolic self-destruction? The intensity with which James punishes any show of masculinity in his little boys would seem to lend credence to such conjecture. Whatever the source of his feelings about male children, the fact of their consistent extermination must be taken into account in any observation of his treatment of children in his fiction.

There is one notable exception to this characteristic view of the doomed male-child as opposed to the transcendent girl-child-cum-adolescent; it is to be found in a tale curiously atypical of James's later phase. With Effie Bream, the child in *The Other House*,[12] James returns once more and for the last time, to the victimized, sacrificial infant with a violence of presentation that surprises as much as it interests the student of his fiction. He recorded the idea in a notebook entry dated December 26,

11. James, *Notes of a Son and Brother*, p. 228.
12. Henry James, *The Other House* (New York, 1947).

1893, then proceeded to make it into a three act play, which was never produced. In May, 1896, he began to fashion it into a novel. It was serialized in the *News* from July 4 to September 26, 1896, and published in book form in two editions in 1896 and 1897.

In this melodramatic tale of a vow given by a husband to his dying wife that he will never remarry after her death as long as their child lives, little Effie is pivotal to the action. Her mother's aggression having turned the child into a pawn, the infant becomes the focal point for a fierce struggle that develops between the "good" and "bad" heroines for possession of her father. As with Dolcino Ambient, the child is the instrument of adult aggression, and her death brings about the denouement that is both tragic and regenerative for the adults who figure in Effie's brief life.

Although fundamental to the action, Effie is sketchily drawn; she is used metaphorically throughout the novel. She emerges more like an object of doom than a real child. Effie, because of her youth, is a mere object in a sinister adult game; she leaves us strangely unmoved despite the enormity of the violence done to her. Yet she is more than thematically important in the novel; she is technically significant. James has made Effie into a poetic device. The physical struggle between Rose, the "bad" heroine, and Jean, the "good" heroine, which takes place in Mrs. Beever's garden, becomes a metaphor for the essential conflict between the two young women and the dead wife for possession of the child's father: "Effie's reach towards her friend [Jean] was so effective that, with Vidal's obligation to rise, it enabled her to slip from his hands and rush to avail herself of the embrace offered her. . . . Rose, however, at the sight of this movement, was quicker than Jean to catch her; she seized her almost with violence, and, holding her as she had held her before, dropped again upon the bench and presented her as a yielding captive." (*Other House*, p. 157)

The conversation between the two women concerns the mundane matter of whether it is time for Effie to be taken home, but the imagery suggests the combative nature of the situation and the magnitude of what is at stake:

> "I only came for the little girl." She turned back to Rose. "I'm afraid it's time I should take her home."
> Rose sat there like a queen-regent with a baby sovereign on her knee. "Must I give her up to you?"
> "I'm responsible for her, you know, to Gorham," Jean returned.
> Rose gravely kissed her little ward, who, now that she was apparently to be offered the entertainment of a debate in which she was so closely concerned, was clearly prepared to contribute to it the calmness of impartial beauty at a joust. (*Other House*, p. 158)

An ironic dimension is added by the child's failure to intuit the danger and her impotence despite her powerful position; the "baby sovereign" is, after all, in the hands of the "queen-regent" and the "impartial beauty at the joust" is destined to be the victim not the judge of the combat.

Effie is referred to as "poor lamb" on several occasions, and the notion of sacrifice is repeatedly associated with her. James sounds the sacrificial note at the beginning of the novel in the following exchange between Jean and Rose:

> "If you'd like, all the same, to see Effie," she [Rose] obligingly added, "I'll so far sacrifice myself as to get her for you?"
> Jean smiled as if this pleasantry were contagious. "You won't sacrifice *her?*"
> Rose Armiger stared. "I won't destroy her." (*Other House*, p. 10)

Later in the novel, when Tony explains his little daughter's absence from the party in honor of her fourth birthday, the imagery succeeds in establishing the sacrificial nature of the child's role:

> "She had been bedizened from top to toe, and then, on some slight appearance of being less well, had been despoiled, denuded and disappointed. She's a poor little lamb of sacrifice. They were at her again, when I came away, with the ribbons and garlands; but there was apparently much more to come, and I couldn't answer for it that a single sneeze wouldn't again lay everything low. It's in the bosom of the gods." (*Other House*, p. 103)

Mrs. Beever remarks that her confrontation with Jean Martle "won't indeed be a scene for that poor lamb!"

All major characters use the sacrificial image in reference to Effie at some point during the course of the novel.

Most successful is James's metaphorical use of the child in the scene after Rose learns of Jean's refusal to marry Paul Beever. Rose's passionate sense of frustration is displaced to the child. Effie becomes the object of the disparate feelings raging in the distraught young woman:

> "She's magnificent!" Rose ardently echoed. "Aren't you, my very own?" she demanded of the child with a sudden passion of tenderness.
> "What did he mean about her wanting the Doctor? She'll see us *all* through—every blessed one of us!" Dennis gave himself up to his serious interest, an odd, voracious manner of taking her in from top to toe.
> "You look at her like an ogre!" Rose laughed, moving away from him with her burden and pressing to her lips as she went a little plump pink arm. She pretended to munch it; she covered it with kisses; she gave way to the joy of her renounced abstention. (*Other House*, p. 154)

Rose's "abstention" stemmed from fear of her own destructive urge toward the child. She had rationalized her coldness to Effie by convincing herself that her behavior was highly ethical; she would never seek Tony's approval by courting his small daughter. But once her situation became hopeless, once she was forced to accept the fact of Jean's selfless love for Tony and the implications of it for herself, the floodgate of her passion was opened and an upsurge of conflicting feelings engulfed her.

The final confrontation between Rose and Jean is again couched in terms of violent struggle for possession of Effie. Jean confesses that her love for the child is rooted in her love for the father:

> "It is because of *that* that I want her!" [says Jean] "Because you adore him—and she's his?" Jean faltered, but she was launched. "Because I adore him—and she's his."

Rose makes one last effort at rationalization:

> "*I* want her for another reason," Rose declared. "I adored her poor mother—and she's hers. That's *my* ground, that's *my* love, that's *my* faith." She caught up Effie again; she held her in two strong arms and dealt her a kiss that was a long consecration. "It's as your dead mother's, my own sweet, that —if it's time—I shall carry you to bed!" (*Other House*, p. 165)

With these words, incredible as it may seem, Rose carries the child off and brutally drowns her. Effie Bream becomes the classical scape-goat, a latter-day sacrificial offering to the undisciplined passions of her elders.

If Effie is the most violently sacrificed of James's victimized children, she is also the last of her species. Another infant was to emerge, phoenix-like, from the ashes of the offering, one destined to live and flourish. The last babe to appear in the novelist's fiction is the little Principino in *The Golden Bowl* (1904). In this final work, the Jamesian hero and heroine for the first time have a child and are presumed, at the denouement, to face a happy and constructive future together. It would appear that by the time he began work on *The Golden Bowl*, James had resolved the inner tensions that had impelled him to create, so consistently, a fictional world in which parents destroy their young. The little Principino figures as a symbol of continuity in familial relations. He never leaves the nursery or the gardens and terraces of Fawns, where "with much pomp and circumstance of perambulator, parasol, fine lace over-veiling and incorruptible female attendance" he takes the air.[13] Yet his presence is indispensable to James's theme; the infant is emblematic of the ideal, the constructive, the enduring, just as the flaw in the bowl (the author's central symbol) represents evil and destruction. The privileged babe has more than material splendour; he has that which James envisioned as a child's birthright—a loving and devoted mother and a father who is "conspicuously addicted to the manipulation of the child in the frank Italian way, at such moments as he judged discreet in respect to other claims." He has, as well, an indulgent and adoring grandfather, whose "visit to his grandson, at some hour or other, held its place, in his day, against all interventions. . . ." For the little Principino the best of American and European traditions of child-rearing have been combined; the warmth and permissiveness of the American parent has been tempered by the discipline and perspective of the European. Although the small son of Maggie Verver and

13. Henry James, *The Golden Bowl* (New York, 1905), p. 109.

Prince Amerigo is peripheral to the main action of the novel, he embodies the notion of ideal childhood, just as the final rapprochement between his parents serves as a model for the ideal marriage.

James's first nameless child of "A Tragedy of Error" was to appear in many guises during the forty years that separated his creation from that of the Principino; he was to suffer much and profoundly at the hands of self-seeking, irresponsible adults; he was to be abused, manipulated, and sacrificed by unscrupulous, heartless parents. In this, his final novel in which a child figures, James was able to project a situation in which all he had sought on behalf of the child is realized. The bleak world of childhood the novelist had depicted throughout his long and productive career is mitigated by his final benign vision of it. But the resolution reflected in *The Golden Bowl* could only have been arrived at after the concentrated focus on problems of childhood and adolescence which characterizes so many of the novels and tales of the preceding decade. The little Principino and his parents emerged only after careful and detailed analysis of cause and effect in child-rearing. James still needed to find a means by which the young could protect themselves in a harsh and cruel adult world. To this end, in the years between 1890 and 1900, James undertook a penetrating study of the young sensibility; and his gift to his persecuted young people was to be the gift of awareness.

CHAPTER V

The "Expanding Consciousness"

The precocious children we have come to associate with Henry James's best-known stories of childhood and adolescence were created within the decade between 1890 and 1900. During these years they moved from the periphery to the very center of the dramatic action in his stories and took command of his fictional scene. But the novelist had long had thematic and technical interest in the inner life of children. In an early tale, "Gabrielle De Bergerac" (1869) (*Complete Tales*, Vol. II), he presented the events of the story through the eyes of an old man recalling his childhood impressions of the love affair and subsequent marriage of his aunt and his tutor. The childhood memories are modified by the intervening consciousness of the aged narrator. The child is thus a narrator-in-retrospect, a clumsy and circuitous device that fails to achieve the historical quality James sought. Much of what the child witnesses could not credibly have come within his field of observation, and the author resorts to unconvincing manipulation to justify the little boy's presence at crucial moments. Nevertheless, the story shows how early in his career James sought the eye-view of childhood.

The child, as seen by the mature man he becomes, is rendered in conventionally romantic terms. He is "listless," "languid," "frail"; his beloved tutor is a devotee of Rousseau, whose educational philosophy James seems to accept at this time without question. He admires the permissive and carefree relationship between master and pupil. It would be many years before the novelist, in the process of working out his own educational philosophy, would question the advisability of complete "permissiveness." Young Bergerac is innocent in his wisdom, voicing verities that disturb the adults around him and inspire his devoted young aunt to hug him and exclaim, "The truth comes out of the mouth of children." Unfortunately, the little Chevalier De Bergerac never comes alive. Twenty years after this awkward attempt to expose adult frailty through the naïve perception of a child, James was able to handle an analogous theme with complete success—"The Pupil," which first appeared in *Longman's Magazine*, March–April, 1891. (*Complete Tales*, VII)

In his preface to Volume XI of the New York Edition, the author tells us that the idea for "The Pupil" was given him by an American doctor residing in Florence. The doctor mentioned an "American family, an odd adventurous, extravagant band of high but rather unauthenticated pretensions, the most interesting member of which was a small boy, acute and precocious, afflicted with a heart of weak action, but beautifully intelligent, who saw their prowling precarious life exactly as it was, and measured and judged it . . . and . . . *them*, all round. . . ." [1]

Morgan Moreen of "The Pupil" is the first of James's important young "seers." The novelist shifts the dramatic action into the consciousness of the eleven-year-old boy, but we see the events through the eyes of the boy's young tutor. Morgan's perceptions are, as it were, filtered through the consciousness of Pemberton, who is, in turn, affected by them. The young tutor is, to some extent, a male counterpart of the governess in "The Turn of the Screw," of a later date. Both have children "pushed off" on them and both take their obligation seriously. At first glance seemingly different in their response to the children entrusted to their care, they do, in fact, share a common weakness vis-à-vis the youngsters. Because they are both unformed and naïve, they cannot serve as competent guides to their charges. Like the governess, Pembroke is immature. He has spent his income in one year "putting his tiny patrimony into a single wave of experience. He had had his full wave, but he couldn't pay his hotel bill."

1. Henry James, *The Art of the Novel*, ed. R. P. Blackmur (New York, 1934), p. 151.

Although he had come down from the university with honors, his timidity, nervousness, and general lack of stability prevented him from realizing his potential. Pemberton's behavior shows a marked failure of perception as to the real situation that exists in the household of which he becomes a part, possibly because there is a touch of the Moreen penchant for self delusion in him.

However, while the governess fails to gain even a modicum of perspective, Pemberton, under the guidance of little Morgan, eventually gains partial insight. The tutor is sensitive and intelligent, but his lack of maturity renders him inadequately prepared for the situation in which he becomes involved. Morgan undertakes to educate him to the actuality of the sordid world of his family. In spite of young Morgan's effort, his tutor only comes to understand the superficial and more obvious aspects of the situation. He never fully grasps the complexity of the child's feelings. Pemberton's young charge is "altogether different from the obvious little Anglo-Saxons who had misrepresented childhood to him." Thus the tutor's initial bewilderment serves as a foil for Morgan's perspicacity. The child "sees" deeply what the tutor at first only faintly senses and later only partially comprehends. As Morgan "places" them for him, the Moreens are fully exposed. Like the governess, the tutor winds up with a dead child on his hands; in this instance, indecisiveness rather than aggression plays a part in the child's death. In "The Pupil" as well as in "The Turn of the Screw," little boys forfeit their lives for the "crime" of self-assertion, for their self-concept as little men, which their immature mentors fail to perceive.

Morgan pays for his insight by experiencing the pain of awareness. He sees that his parents are irresponsible adventurers whose turpitude stands in direct contrast to his own innate sense of decency. The burden of his shame is heavy. Essentially this is a tale in which James gives expression—through the eyes of Morgan and ultimately through those of his tutor—to his most firmly held convictions about the quality of family relations. By extension he is commenting, as well, on the false standards and shoddy values of a world that places "appearance" above human feeling.

In his preface to the tale, James explained that he had not fully developed his portrait of Morgan's family: "The Moreens were of the family then of the great unstudied precursors—poor and shabby members, no doubt; dim and superseded types. I must add indeed that, such as they were, or as they may at present incoherently appear, I don't pretend really to have 'done' them; all I have given in 'The Pupil' is little Morgan's troubled vision of them as reflected in the vision, also troubled enough, of his devoted friend."[2]

The novelist had no need to make excuses for his rendering of the Moreens. The reader responds to every nuance of the child's complicated relation with them. To see Mrs. Moreen for the first time, as James makes us see her, is to know her instantly. The reader first meets her as she seeks to engage Pemberton as tutor to her son. James has captured the shoddy quality of the woman and the system of values by which she lives: ". . . the large, affable lady . . . sat there drawing a pair of soiled *gants de Suède* through a fat, jewelled hand and, at once pressing and gliding, repeated over and over everything but the thing he [Pemberton] would have liked to hear. He would have liked to hear the figure of his salary. . . ." (*Complete Tales*, VII, 409)

Mrs. Moreen's ethics are like her soiled gloves. She is essentially indifferent to anyone who does not further her pathetic aspiration to be part of a world in which she has no place. "Pemberton saw on a nearer view that her elegance was intermittent and her parts didn't always match." Morgan's mother has several dimensions, and James presents her in all her complexity. He captures her shrewdness and the surface amiability that covers a sinister disregard for all but the public image she desperately tries to create: "[Pemberton] could trace perfectly the degrees by which, in proportion as her little son confined himself to his tutor for society, Mrs. Moreen shrewdly forbore to renew his garments. She did nothing

2. Ibid., p. 153.

that didn't show, neglected him because he escaped notice, and then, as he illustrated this clever policy, dis-
couraged at home his public appearances. Her position
was logical enough—those members of her family who
did show had to be showy." (*Complete Tales*, VII, 423)

Her shrewd calculation that Pemberton would come to
care too much for Morgan to desert him, thus taking responsibility for the child without remuneration, is as
chilling an exhibition of parental irresponsibility as one
could imagine. Yet there is something pathetic about
Mrs. Moreen. The upsurge of faith before every sally into
the *monde chic*, the terrible deflation of all hope after the
inevitable defeat of each thrust inspires pity for the futility of her aspirations. In the scene when she desperately tries to borrow sixty francs from the tutor whom
she has not paid in a year, the reader as well as Pemberton is moved to "a fantastic, demoralized sympathy with
her."

Mr. Moreen and his older son, Ulick, are "men of the
world," a term James uses ironically again and again to
designate them throughout the tale. Like the ribbon of an
unnamed foreign order which Mr. Moreen wears in his
buttonhole, bestowed for services never specified, his
"worldliness" is sham. He is rendered in terms of the
ephemeral in order to accentuate that aspect of the family's position. We never learn what he does, that is from
what source he derives his income; he "looks out" for the
family by going off to unspecified places to engage in un-
designated ventures; we do know that he is at all times
the "cosmopolite." When Pemberton confronts him with
the fact that he has not been paid in a year, "Mr. Moreen
. . . listen[s] to him as he listen[s] to every one and
every thing, like a man of the world. . . ." When he gives
Pemberton three hundred francs under duress, he presents them to him "again with all the precaution of a man
of the world." He appeals to the tutor "as usual, as a man
of the world" not to tell Morgan of his ungentlemanly behavior. When Morgan and Pemberton decide that the tutor must leave the family and take a position which will
guarantee subsistence. "Mr. Moreen and Ulick . . . when,

on coming in, *they* heard the cruel news, they took it like perfect men of the world." In the final passage of the tale Mr. Moreen's reaction to little Morgan's death is the epitaph for the child's relations with his family: "[Mr. Moreen] was trembling all over, and he was, in his way, as deeply affected as his wife. But, after the first, he took his bereavement like a man of the world." (*Complete Tales*, VII, 460)

Because they live in a mist of self-delusion, the Moreens have no identity. The sentient child, in search of his own selfhood, comes face to face with this inescapable truth about his family: "I don't know what they live on, or how they live, or *why* they live! What have they got and how did they get it? . . . Who are they, any way, and what are they? I've thought of all that—I've thought of a lot of things. They're so beastly worldly. That's what I hate most—Oh, I've *seen* it!" (*Complete Tales*, VII, 438)

In the context of this tale, worldliness and makeshift cosmopolitanism take on a negative, almost sinister coloration. The tale implies that worldliness, rooted in snobbery and sought at the expense of responsibility, can be destructive of the whole fabric of society. Family, and ultimately social relations, can only be sound when concern for the emotional and spiritual well-being of the individual is the concern and responsibility of all. True social consciousness lies in interested, ethical, and moral behavior on the part of parents to children; such behavior assures the proper response from the young. A world where roles are reversed, where a child becomes the judge of his elders and must assume the responsibility for creating a healthy moral climate for himself is indeed a topsy-turvy world. The whole complex of familial relationships is illuminated through the consciousness of the precocious little boy.

The child's precocity turns him into a "man-child": "Pemberton . . . glanced at him as he walked slowly to the window with his back turned, his hands in his pockets and the air in his elderly shoulders of a boy who didn't play." (*Complete Tales*, VII, 411) James insists upon this image of Morgan. Pemberton notices that there is "something rather elderly and gentlemanly in Morgan's seediness—it differed from the untidiness of the urchin who plays and spoils his things." And again, "It was as if he had been a little gentleman and had paid the penalty by discovering that he was the only such person in the family." In one of the few early references to James's fictional children, Pelham Edgar saw Morgan as "preternaturally precocious and prematurely diseased." He goes on to remark that "there are only four children whom I remember, and each is presented to us as an abnormality."[3] Early critics, when they discussed James's children, failed to appreciate the extent to which the novelist anticipated modern psychology in his concern with the effects of parental indifference on a supersensitive child.

"It was strange," mused Pemberton, "how they [the Moreens] contrived to reconcile the appearance and indeed the essential fact, of adoring the child with their eagerness to wash their hands of him. Did they want to get rid of him before he should find them out?" Because of his gift of perception and his innate ethical sense, Morgan is indeed a burden to his improvident parents, and, in spite of their protestations of love, they reject him with a finality that breaks his heart. He begins to understand this at an early age, and the strain of living with it becomes the matrix in which his curiously superannuated personality is formed:

"My darling, you're too quaint!" his mother exclaimed, putting out to caress him a practiced but ineffectual hand. He slipped out of it, but looked with intelligent, innocent eyes at Pemberton, who already had time to notice that from one moment to the other his small satiric face seemed to change its time of life. At this moment it was infantine; yet it appeared also to be under the influence of curious intuitions and knowledges. (*Complete Tales*, VII, 411)

Morgan Moreen is not a "realistically" rendered child. He is an essence, the embodiment of an aware and troubled conscience pitted against the blind, corrupt cynicism of parental dereliction; like Dolcino before him and Miles after, he is doomed to die of it. In his relation to his

3. Pelham Edgar, *Henry James, Man and Author* (Toronto, 1927), p. 125.

parents he dramatizes the ironic and paradoxical reversal of roles. The moral strength and example that should be demonstrated by the parental guide has, in fact, been taken over by the child. James has heightened his characterization of the boy. Thematically it was necessary for Morgan to have "the general quality of a child for whom life had not been simplified by school, a kind of home-bred sensibility which might have been bad for himself but was charming for others, and a whole range of refinement and perception—little musical vibrations as taking as picked up airs . . . at the same time he had in his composition a sharp spice of stoicism, doubtless the fruit of having had to begin early to bear pain, which produced the impression of pluck." The characterization of Morgan is amplified but plausible. More than in Dolcino or Miles, we recognize in him one possible response on the part of a sensitive child to parental indifference and rejection.

In spite of the ambiguities in the tale in which he figures, little Miles of "The Turn of the Screw" (*Complete Tales*, X) is concretely presented. The boy is alert and "aware"; the question becomes, precisely, what it is he is aware of. Miles is remarkably perceptive and intelligent. For all her hysteria, the governess is impressed by "his perpetually striking show of cleverness." She sees him as "extraordinarily sensitive," yet this becomes, oddly enough, proof of his wickedness for her. Despite the fact that our impression of Miles is derived from the governess' subjective view of him, the reader cannot help but admire the child's understanding of himself and of the adults around him. When the governess—convinced that he has gone out in the dead of night to meet the ghost of Peter Quint—asks him why he left the house, he counters with "If I tell you why, will you understand?" The governess misinterprets the child's question. She believes that what she must "understand" is his relation with Peter Quint. Actually the child wonders whether she will understand that children are sometimes naughty in order to get attention from adults. It is quite conceivable that the orphaned little boy, irresponsibly abandoned by his uncle, would have an excessive need for such evidence of concern on the part of the adult responsible for him. Remarkable is his sense of his own need. He tells the governess that he did it "well . . . just exactly in order that you should do this [come looking for him]."

While Miles shares Morgan Moreen's capacity for intuitive perception, he does not have his predecessor's adult insight. In fact, James keeps little Miles brilliantly boyish. "And you can't say I've not been awfully good, can you? . . . except just that one night, you know . . . when I went down—went out of the house . . . to show you I could . . . and can again." These are the words of a small boy pleading for something he wants very much. One is consistently aware of the child behind Miles's grown-up behavior and precocious diction. This serves to intensify the reader's feeling of sympathy for the bright, sensitive youngster who is trying to cope as best he can with an adult making extraordinary demands upon him. Since the governess never states explicitly what it is she is demanding of him, the child is forced to rely on his intuition. Like any boy his age, he is eager to expand his horizon, to be with his male peers—"I want to see more of life. I want my own sort." But more than this, the youngster senses the governess' strange reluctance to give him up. In her fierce possessiveness he divines a threat that can only be met with manly resistance. He therefore resolves to settle with her the problem of his future education. The young woman's distraught reaction when he raises the question on the way to church further bewilders and discomforts the child. He begins to appreciate the gravity of his situation:

> "Then you weren't asleep?" [the governess asks that evening]
> "Not much! I lie awake and think." [Miles replies]
> "What is it . . . that you think of?"
> "What in the world, my dear, but *you*. . . . I think also, you know, of this queer business of ours . . . the way you bring me up. And all the rest!" (*Complete Tales*, X, 101–2)

The hasty departure of Flora, accompanied by Mrs. Grose, increases his apprehension and intensifies his resolve to "clear the air." He feels that, like his small sister, he must get away from the governess. Yet, in his final confrontation with her, he makes his bid for freedom with tact and manly dignity. Asked if he had been expelled from school for stealing, he "very simply" replies "No, I did not steal." Asked directly for an explanation of his expulsion, he answers directly that he "said things." "Only that?" the governess demands. "They thought it was enough!" is his firm, mature reply. Miles is determined to face what needs to be faced and to deal with it. But the governess' response to the boy's manly posture is negative. Because of the nature of her attachment to Miles, the young woman feels threatened by his self-assertiveness. Behind the governess' frantic effort to subdue and possess Miles lies a sexual fantasy that is made explicit at the beginning of the scene:

We continued silent while the maid was with us—as silent, it whimsically occurred to me, as some young couple who, on their wedding-journey, at the inn, feel shy in the presence of the waiter. He turned round only when the waiter had left us. "Well—so we're alone!" (*Complete Tales*, X, 128)

As long as the boy remained a passive, asexual child, the governess could control her anxiety over the forbidden fantasy. Once she feels Miles as a sexual presence, she is overwhelmingly threatened; the fantasy becomes a frightening reality. And so the terrified governess pushes the child to the last extremity: "He almost smiled at me in the desolation of his surrender, which was indeed practically, by this time, so complete that I ought to have left it there. But I was infatuated—I was blind with victory. . . ." (*Complete Tales*, X, 136)

Determined to destroy any vestige of masculinity in him, the governess literally frightens Miles to death with her evocation of the ghost of Peter Quint. But not before the boy has "seen," with a terrible lucidity, the lengths to which the young woman entrusted with his care would go in order to deprive him of his manhood. It was more than the trapped child could sustain; "his little heart, dispossessed, had stopped." And yet another Jamesian boy-child has paid with his life for his vision of freedom.

It has by now become clear that little boys rarely live

to achieve manhood in James's fiction. Both Morgan and Miles are destroyed in acts of self-assertion. The mere thought of freedom kills Morgan; masculine self-affirmation destroys Miles. Mature sexuality is denied the novelist's boy-children. Even passive, unknowing little Dolcino Ambient is a victim of what is basically his mother's sexual anxiety. While most of these male children perceive the adult aggression directed toward them, they lack the physical strength to profit from their insight; they are unable to stand up to the strain of becoming men.

At the same time that James imagined Dolcino, Morgan, and little Miles, he was creating a new child, a girl-child equipped to deal with the adult world, one capable of protecting herself by doing more than distinguish between the excellent and the base, the real and the unreal; he was creating a child with the physical and moral stamina necessary to attain maturity, a child who would put its perceptions to work in creating a better world in which to live. With his transcendent girl-child, James arrived at his distinctive educational philosophy as well as a resolution of his ambivalent attitude toward the American-European polarity that had for so long dominated his intellectual and emotional life.

CHAPTER VI

Educational Theory
and the Jeune Fille

James's educational theory evolved, in no small degree, from his interest in the French manner of rearing the *jeune fille*. The notion of the protected young girl had long appealed to the novelist. The education of the French young female supplied in abundance that which James had missed in his own childhood—clearly defined expectations on the part of parents as evidence of their concern. He tells us in his autobiography, ". . . our 'fending' . . . for ourselves didn't so prepare us for invidious remark . . . as to hush in my breast the appeal to our parents, not for religious instruction (of which we had plenty, and of the most charming and familiar) but simply for instruction (a very different thing) as to where we should say we 'went,' in our world, under cold scrutiny or derisive comment."[1] Henry James, Senior, who was nothing if not eclectic in his attitude toward the education of his children, replied that "there was no communion, even that of the Catholics, even that of the Jews, even that of the Swedenborgians, from which we need find ourselves excluded." Unlimited freedom of choice is disconcerting to small children and young Henry's response was predictable: "I not only failed quite to rise to the parental reasoning, but made out in it rather a certain sophistry; such a prevarication for instance as if we had habitually said we kept the carriage we observedly didn't keep, kept it because we sent when we wanted one to Uni-

1. Henry James, *A Small Boy and Others* (New York, 1913), pp. 233, 34.

versity Place, where Mr. Hathorn had his livery-stable." [2]

Carefully nurtured European children were not faced with the dilemma of finding their own answers to crucial questions. They knew exactly where they "went," who they were, what was expected of them. Young James, on the other hand, "breathed inconsistency and ate and drank contradiction." [3] Yet, in retrospect, he perceived advantages in the liberal attitude of his parents. "No education," he remarked in adulthood, "avails for the intelligence that doesn't stir in it some subjective passion." [4] The fact that his freedom brought him a measure of uncertainty did not diminish the pleasure he derived from opportunities to observe people and things around him. The James family traveled extensively during the novelist's formative years, and he often found himself taking in the social scene from the "exhibition-stage of the piazza" of a fashionable hotel: ". . . of so entrancing an interest did I feel it at the time to *be* an hotel child, and so little would I have exchanged my lot with that of any small person more privately bred. . . . For there, incomparably, was the chance to dawdle and gape.[5]

If restriction offered security, freedom offered license. Unfortunately, however, small children infer parental indifference from an excess of freedom, and it was difficult for the little boy to reconcile his need for established limits with his need for unfettered opportunities. Thus the essential conflict and ambivalence that found expression in James's fiction—the American versus the European "way"—may well have had its inception in his own educational experience in childhood.

As James sought to reconcile Europe and America, so he gradually, over the years, effected a reconciliation between the "natural" and "artificial" approaches to child-rearing. This reconciliation evolved over a long period of observing and studying European and American manners and it necessitated, as well, the mastery of conflicting

2. Ibid., p. 235.
3. Ibid., p. 216.
4. Ibid., p. 26.
5. Ibid., p. 30.

impulses engendered in his own childhood. In 1913, at the age of seventy, he wrote of his youthful impressions:

> . . . if we saw the "natural" so happily embodied about us—and in the female maturity or comparative maturity, scarce less than in female adolescence—this was because the artificial or in other words the complicated, was so little there to threaten it. . . . We came more or less to see that our young contemporaries of another world, the trained and admonished, the disciplined and governessed, or in a word the formed, relatively speaking, had been made aware of many things of which those at home hadn't been; yet we were also to note . . . that, the awareness in question remaining at best imperfect, our little friends . . . advanced and presumed but to flounder and recede, elated at once and abashed and on the whole but *feebly* sophisticated.[6]

The polarities we associate with James's representation of the international scene—innocence versus sophistication, good versus evil, an old traditional society versus a new rootless one—are implicit in his handling of the epistemological theme. Indeed, his theory of education is so much a part of his world view that we cannot separate the one from the other. He resolved his American-European dilemma by creating a fictional world in which the drawing rooms of both countries served as arena for a clash of universal human values; and he created his own *jeune fille*, the synthesis of all that was acceptable to him in the "natural" as well as in the "artificial" educational process.

In 1876, while on holiday in Etretat, a French resort, the young author was first struck by "the immense difference between the lot of the *jeune fille* and her American sister." He incorporated his impressions in a travel sketch:

> People went about in compact, cohesive groups. . . . The groups usually formed a solid phalanx around two or three young girls, compressed into the centre, the preservation of whose innocence was their chief solicitude. . . . I used to pity the young ladies at first, for this perpetual application of the leading-string; but a little reflection showed me that the French have ordered this as well as they have ordered everything else . . . if French marriages are almost always arranged, it must be added that they are in the majority of cases arranged successfully. Therefore, if a *jeune fille* is for three or

6. Ibid., pp. 54, 55.

four years tied with a very short rope and compelled to browse exclusively upon the meagre herbage which sprouts in the maternal shadow, she has at least the comfort of reflecting that . . . measures are being carefully taken to promote her to a condition of unbounded liberty.[7]

The key to the success of the French system was, for James, the position of the mother in the hierarchy of the family. "To be a *mère de famille*," he continued, "is to occupy not simply (as is mostly the case with us) a sentimental, but really an official position." The French mother controlled the destiny of her daughter and was obligated to pass the legacy of power on to her. Such responsibility requires strength and selfless dedication, qualities that, for James, were inseparable from the parental function. The travel sketch is significant not only because we recognize in his comments on the *jeune fille* the genesis of Daisy Miller, Pansy Osmond, Nanda Brookenham, and Jeanne de Vionnet but because it adumbrates one of James's recurrent themes dealing with family relations—the necessity for parental responsibility.

James's view of the French mother as powerful and devoted was one he retained all his life. In *The Ambassadors* (1903), Miss Gostry remarks to Lambert Strether of Madame de Vionnet, "You must remember that of her—that as a mother she's French, and that for them there's a special providence." [8] That is why Jeanne de Vionnet, James's last *jeune fille*, is "bright gentle shy happy wonderful." Her unusual mother has given her the best of both worlds. "Oh but I'm almost American too," says Jeanne to Strether, "That's what mamma has wanted me to be—I mean *like* that; for she has wanted me to have lots of freedom. She has known such good results from it." [9] Jeanne is "an exquisite case of education," possible because of her mother's rare combination of strength and sensitivity. When James's own mother died in 1882, he made the following entry in his notebook:

It was a perfect mother's life—the life of a perfect wife. To bring her children into the world—to expend herself, for

7. Henry James, *Portraits of Places* (Boston, 1885), pp. 163–64.
8. Henry James, *The Ambassadors* (New York, 1964), p. 140.
9. Ibid., p. 154.

years, for their happiness and welfare—then, when they had reached a full maturity and were absorbed in the world and in their own interests—to lay herself down in her ebbing strength and yield up her pure soul to the celestial power that had given her this divine commission. Thank God one knows this loss but once; and thank God that certain supreme impressions remain.[10]

Leon Edel remarks that the images her children used to describe Mary James convey an impression "of an august and omniscient personage walking with unheard step through a household where justice and mercy had to be dispensed even-handed and with generosity among contending factions . . . a figure devoted and loyal, vigilant and unrelaxed." [11] The strong, dedicated mother is what, in the French educational system, appealed most to James, appealed to that aspect of his personality which felt the need for parental guidance. But of the other Henry James, the sentient observer, the perceptive advocate of "the felt life," there is another story to be told.

Conflict between James's craving for limitation and his impulse to accumulate unlimited experience found expression in his fictional representation of the young girl. The discrepancy between the novelist's nonfictional statements about the *jeune fille* and his finished portraits of adolescent girls stems from his own insatiable need to "see" and "know" all that life had to offer. Without awareness there could be no existence for him. Unfortunately, awareness brought with it the recognition of evil and exposure to it; this in turn threatened contamination. The problem of the relationship between knowledge of evil and moral excellence was to occupy James for nearly three decades. Early in his career it found fictional expression in Daisy Miller, created in 1878 (two years after his observations on the French *jeune fille*) and in his representation of Pansy Osmond in *The Portrait of a Lady* in 1881. Between 1881 and 1889, it was to be reflected in novels, tales, and notebook entries, as well.

On January 17, 1881, James recorded the idea that was

10. *The Notebooks of Henry James*, ed. F. O. Matthiessen and Kenneth B. Murdock (New York, 1962), p. 41.
11. Leon Edel, *Henry James*, Vol I. *The Untried Years: 1843–1870* (New York, 1953), p. 41.

to develop into "The Impressions of a Cousin": "I heard an allusion yesterday to a matter in the history of Mme de Sévigné, which suggested the germ of a story . . . her unbecoming conduct in siding with her daughter against the poor little *demoiselle de Grignan,* who was being forced into a convent, because her father, during her minority, had spent all her property and didn't wish to have to give an account of it." [12]

James retained the basic idea of the father who forces the girl into a convent. He added the following: "To his surprise—though he has strong reason to believe that she suspects his infidelity (she must yet be in her minority), she consents with great meekness [to go into the convent]. . . . He then tries to keep her . . . from retiring from the world. . . . But she persists, with the same sad gentleness and turns away from him forever.[13]

As the character of the young girl begins to take form for James, she cannot escape awareness; she may renounce the world, retire from it into a convent, but she will do so with full knowledge of its wickedness. By the time "The Impressions of a Cousin" appeared in *Century,* November and December of 1883, the little *demoiselle de Grignan* had been transformed into an American girl who understands the situation, does not go into a convent, and, by implication, may even look forward to a satisfactory future. Whatever her fate, James could not bring himself to cut her off from experience.

The novelist's complex attitude toward the question of the education of the young girl is exemplified in a series of notebook entries that extend over a period of seven years; they deal with the theme of a story he never wrote:

August 4, 1892

Last evening, at Ouchy, Miss R. said, after the conversation had run a little upon the way Americans drag their children about Europe: "A girl should be shown Europe—or taken to travel—by her husband—she has no business to see the world before. *He* takes her—*he* initiates her."

Struck with this as the old-fashioned French view and pos-

12. *Notebooks,* p. 19.
13. Ibid., p. 20.

sible idea for a little tale. The girl whose husband is to show her everything—so she waits at home—and who never gets a husband. *He* is to take her abroad—and he never comes, etc. The daughter of a conservative "frenchified" mother etc. A pretext for the mother's selfishness, neglect, etc.—*she* travelling about. The girl's life—waiting—growing older—death. The husband comes in the form of death, etc.[14]

The passage is richly connotative. Not only did the novelist see marriage as a form of extinction, but the sheltered life suggested death of the developing sensibility to him. In a December 21, 1895, entry he included the motif in a list of possible ideas for a tale: "The mother who takes the line that her daughter's husband must show her everything—the husband never comes." Three years later (May 7, 1898) the idea was still with him: "Etta R.'s case of maturing, withering daughter. 'Her *husband* will *show* her the world, travel with her—a girl—in *our monde*—waits for *that*.' "[15] In the fourth and final notebook reference to the theme it becomes clear why James never made a tale of it:

October 5, 1899
. . . the little thing noted a long time ago as on a word dropped by Miss R.—the way for a woman (girl) to see the world, to travel, being for her husband to show her. The foreignized American mother who takes that line—the *un*-foreignized ditto—or, rather, American girl herself—who represents the idea of the young woman putting in all she can *before*—either to show it herself to her husband, or because she will, *after*, with the shelved and effaced state of so many, precisely, *by* marriage, have no chance. I might give the 3 images: the girl *à la* Miss Reubel (I mean evoked by her word); and the 1st and second, *both*, of these last-mentioned cases. They would make a little presented "scenic" trio.[16]

The story of the young girl who waits to be shown Europe was never written because James had already made his statement on the theme in several novels and tales of the 1880's and 1890's.

In 1891, one year before James's first notebook entry about the girl to whom seclusion brings death, "The Chaperon" appeared in the *Atlantic Monthly*. His heroine is one of the young women he was to envision for his

14. Ibid., p. 125.
15. Ibid., p. 266.
16. Ibid., p. 295.

"scenic trio." With Rose Tramore, James was well on his way toward a resolution of the problem of the *jeune fille* and the "exposed" young woman. Rose is "pretty, with charm, clever, quietly resolute, reticent and imperturable," all qualities that would characterize the Jamesian *jeune fille*. The concept of the ideal young girl had crystalized for him; it remained only for the author to give his heroine the full-length treatment the novel form could afford. Between 1881, when he created Pansy Osmond, and 1899, when he conceived of Nanda Brookenham, James had explored every facet of the perceptive, curious young girl in such tales as "Pandora," "A London Life," "The Patagonia," "The Turn of the Screw," and "In the Cage." By the time he made his last notebook reference to the theme of the sheltered daughter and the "frenchified" mother, he had already produced two novels based on this motif—*What Maisie Knew* and *The Awkward Age*. The notebook entries of the unwritten tale are of singular interest because they serve as a gloss to the course he was actually taking in his fiction; we discern in them the evolution of the girl-heroines he *did* create.

The notebook entries illuminate, as well, James's attitude toward marriage in America. In a travel sketch of 1876 he expressed the view that for American women marriage meant "being socially shelved—and it is not too much to say, in certain circles, degraded." [17] His notebook entry of 1899 demonstrates that his opinion had not changed in the intervening twenty-three years. This suggests that the theme of the reversal of roles between parent and child which he was to introduce again and again is rooted in his feeling about the position of the married woman in American society. James's nonfictional remarks on the American mother imply that social attitudes encourage her to evade maternal responsibility. Because the American mother (unlike the *mère de famille*) was relegated to a position of weakness within the family constellation, her daughter was forced to fend for herself. In spite of his conviction that this was a real-

17. *Portraits of Places*, p. 164.

ity of the American educational situation, James had difficulty accepting it. Consequently two young heroines struggled for ascendance in the novelist's fictional world —the active, powerful, aware American girl and the passive, gentle, sheltered European *jeune fille*. He combined the two only after he had experimented, through his young heroines, with the polarities of knowledge and innocence, good and evil, activity and passivity. Although an interest in the education of young girls is evident in his first novel, *Watch and Ward* (1871), it is with Pansy Osmond in *The Portrait of a Lady* that James seriously began the process of fashioning his unique version of the *jeune fille*.[18]

By the time he created Pansy, James had mastered the exploration of character and consciousness which distinguishes his best fictional portraits of children. This carefully nurtured *jeune fille* is conscious of her enforced role as passive actor and active observer. Pansy has a highly developed sensibility that determines her intellectual and emotional coloration. She is conceived in the romantic tradition; great emphasis is placed on her intuitive faculty. This sets her apart from her predecessors as she foreshadows future heroines such as Maisie and Nanda. She is, as well, the first of James's adolescents through whom the novelist directly raises the question of what constitutes a "well-brought-up" girl. Does innocence ensure virtue? What is the relationship between self knowledge and a grasp of the realities of life?

Unlike most of the children who preceded her, Pansy Osmond is a complicated little entity. Like Hyacinth and Verena, indeed like all James's important fictional children, her "conditioning" has determined her character. When the reader first meets her in the garden of her father's villa in Florence, she is fresh from the convent where she has been "impregnated with the idea of submission which was due to any one who took the tone of authority; and she was a passive spectator of the operation of her fate." The submission so painstakingly inculcated in the child has led to an intensification of her

18. Henry James, *The Portrait of a Lady* (New York, 1909).

perceptions. She is dimly aware of a particular relationship between her father and Madame Merle:

> "If we're going to discuss that matter she had better go out of the room." [says her father]
> "Let her stay," said Madame Merle, "We'll talk of something else."
> "If you like I won't listen," Pansy suggested with an appearance of candour which imposed conviction. . . .
> "Go into the garden, *mignonne*, and pluck a flower or two for Madame Merle," [Osmond] went on in French.
> "That's just what I wanted to do," Pansy exclaimed, rising with promptness and noiselessly departing. (*Portrait*, I, 340, 342)

A positive facet of Pansy's submissiveness is the grasp of reality it reflects. The young girl's awareness functions as an ironic comment on Isabel Archer's passage from innocence to knowledge. She is able to exercise judgement where Isabel fails. Pansy and Isabel become emblematic in the novel of two kinds of innocence. Isabel's innocence cannot come to terms with the fact of evil; Pansy's is a wise self-protective innocence, coexisting with an apprehension of evil, the recognition and acceptance of it as part of life. Her restricted childhood encouraged the free play of her imagination, while Isabel, for all her apparent freedom, was a captive of her own lack of vision. Imprisoned in her innocence, Isabel underestimates Pansy as she tragically misjudges Osmond and Madame Merle:

> Isabel wondered at her; she had never had so directly presented to her nose the white flower of cultivated sweetness. How well the child had been taught, said our admiring young woman; how prettily she had been directed and fashioned; and yet how simple, how natural, how innocent she had been kept! Isabel was fond, ever, of the question of character and quality, of sounding, as who should say, the deep personal mystery, and it had pleased her, up to this time, to be in doubt as to whether this tender slip were not really all-knowing. Was the extremity of her candour but the perfection of self-consciousness? Was it put on to please her father's visitor, or was it the direct expression of an unspotted nature? (*Portrait*, II, 26)

There is little room in Isabel's perception of people for shading or nuance; her judgment of them consequently lacks perspective. She cannot imagine evil until it actively enters her life. This want of insight which has such sad consequences for her is evident in her evaluation of Pansy:

> . . . her interview with the daughter of the house . . . effectively settled this question. Pansy was really a blank page, a pure white surface, successfully kept so. She had neither art, nor guile, nor temper, nor talent—only two or three small exquisite instincts: for knowing a friend, for avoiding a mistake, for taking care of an old toy or a new frock. Yet . . . she could be felt as an easy victim of fate. She would have no will, no power to resist, no sense of her own importance; she would easily be mystified, easily crushed: her force would be all in knowing when and where to cling. (*Portrait*, II, 26)

This view of the younger girl is perhaps valid but Isabel fails to see her own affinity with the child. Ironically Isabel's analysis of Pansy holds true not only for the child but also for herself. Much later, after her own awakening, Isabel realizes that it is she who is "an easy victim of fate." The heroine of *The Portrait*, like her young step-daughter, has "no will, no power to resist, no sense of her own importance." It is she who is "easily mystified, easily crushed" by her failure to have understood, before it was too late, the true nature of the man she married. Pansy is not shocked to learn that most of the important people in her life are selfish, immoral, and hypocritical. She had known what there was to know for a long time, even that her momentary rebellion would be short-lived.

In Pansy, James created the first of a group of fictional children who were to serve as touchstones for adult values. Much is made of her innocence by the grown-ups who surround her. Innocence signifies for each of them a lack of perception, ignorance of the realities of life. The reactions of these people to her innocence (as they understand it) further illuminates and defines them for us. For Madame Merle, Pansy's innocence is a commodity; by selling it to the highest bidder she will realize her own frustrated ambitions. For Isabel this aspect of Pansy's character has purely moral value. For Osmond, his daughter's innocence has merely aesthetic worth; it completes the picture of the perfect *jeune fille*, preserves the compositional arrangement of his domestic work of art: "Isabel was impressed by Osmond's artistic, the plastic view, as it somehow appeared, of Pansy's innocence—her own appreciation of it being more anxiously moral." (*Portrait*, II, 84)

Pansy's seeming unawareness is contrasted with Isabel's show of sophistication. Pansy "sees" and "knows" what Isabel dares not acknowledge—the moral dilemma in which they both find themselves. Isabel has her first indication of Pansy's perception when she urges the girl to consider the match with Lord Warburton, a match distasteful to her but completely desirable to Osmond:

> "Yes, he has been very kind," Pansy answered, "That's what I like him for."
> "Why then [asks Isabel] is the difficulty so great?"
> "I've always felt sure of his knowing that I don't want— what did you say I should do?—to encourage him. He knows that I don't want to marry, and he wants me to know that he therefore won't trouble me. That's the meaning of his kindness. It's as if he said to me: 'I like you very much, but if it does n't please you I'll never say it again.' I think that's very kind, very noble," Pansy went on with deepening positiveness. "That's all we've said to each other. And he does n't care for me either. Ah, no there's no danger." (*Portrait*, II, 259–60)

Pansy senses that Lord Warburton's true motive for wooing her lies in something other than his affection for her. The young girl's grasp of the situation alarms Isabel: "Isabel was touched with wonder at the depths of perception of which this submissive little person was capable; she felt afraid of Pansy's wisdom—began almost to retreat before it." (*Portrait*, II, 260) Pansy's "wisdom" threatens the older woman's sense of reality. Isabel fears the young girl's insight yet she envies and, in an odd way, draws strength from the knowledge that Pansy will be able to cope with her situation:

> "You must tell your father that," she remarked reservedly.
> "I think I'd rather not," Pansy unreservedly answered.
> "You ought n't to let him have false hopes."
> "Perhaps not; but it will be good for me that he should. So long as he believes that Lord Warburton intends anything of the kind you say, papa won't propose anyone else. And that will be an advantage for me," said the child very lucidly.
> There was something brilliant in her lucidity, and it made her companion draw a long breath. It relieved this friend of a heavy responsibility. Pansy had sufficient illumination of her

own, and Isabel felt that she herself just now had no light to spare from her small stock. (*Portrait*, II, 260)

The only thing Pansy wanted in life was to marry "poor Mr. Rosier" with his "genteel" income of forty thousand francs. This Osmond categorically forbade. When Isabel urges the girl to seek a "better" marriage with a man whose fortune is larger, she is "grateful for the dimness of the room; she felt as if her face were hideously insincere." Isabel sees her younger, idealistic self in the girl before her. Her identification with Pansy is evident throughout. It is most marked after her own initiation into the realities of her world. When she decides, against Osmond's will, to go to England to see Ralph Touchett before he dies, her first thought is of Pansy. Isabel's subsequent return to Osmond at the end of the novel is motivated partly by her acceptance of parental responsibility but more importantly by her feeling of kinship with the child. She has learned something from Pansy. The younger girl's submission to "the way things are" foreshadows Isabel's final surrender to the fate she had, after all, freely chosen for herself:

She laid her hand on Pansy's as if to let her know that her look conveyed no diminution of esteem; for the collapse of the girl's momentary resistance . . . seemed only her tribute to the truth of things. She did n't presume to judge others, but she had judged herself; she had seen the reality. She had no vocation for struggling with combinations; in the solemnity of sequestration there was something that overwhelmed her. She bowed her pretty head to authority and only asked of authority to be merciful. (*Portrait*, II, 385)

Just as Pansy bends to the inevitable, so Isabel, in the denouement with Casper Goodwood, realizes that, for her, there is only "a very straight path back" to a servitude less frightening than the liberation offered by her persistent American suitor. Isabel can purchase liberation from the vicious and sterile "good taste" of Osmond only at the price of an erotic involvement with Goodwood. She had always felt that she had passion to give; she had "a belief that if a certain light should dawn, she could give herself completely." But the reality of it alarmed her; it was an image "on the whole too formidable to be attractive." And when in Casper Goodwood's "kiss of white lightening" that "certain light" does dawn, she cannot endure its intensity. Isabel's choice is not between freedom and servitude; it is rather between two extreme and undesirable alternatives. Her clear perception of this links her more closely than ever with Pansy, who has always known that freedom is an illusion.

Because Isabel Archer completely dominates the novel, there has been a tendency on the part of critics to neglect the characterization of Pansy Osmond. James's rendering of the wise little *jeune fille* is exquisite in its detail. But more than this, Pansy is significant in the evolution of the Jamesian child; in his treatment of her we find themes that will be developed in the children who follow and also a tentative statement on the education of the young.

Unlike Pansy, the children of the next decade do more than perceive and submit; they struggle—sometimes in vain—against a hostile adult world characterized by the absence of moral values. During this decade we find the most varied and complex handling of the child in all the novelist's fiction. James tells us in his preface to Volume XI of the New York Edition that "the sensibility of the female young is indubitably, for early youth, the greater. . . ." [19] This is his justification for having chosen a girl-child for his center of consciousness in *What Maisie Knew*.

However, what differentiates James's little girls of this period from their male counterparts is hardly their degree of sentience. They are differentiated by their ultimate fate. Morgan Moreen and little Miles have sensibility in abundance; what they lack is physical strength. The novelist recognized his tendency to endow young females with energy denied young males. Comparing his little boys with Maisie and the telegraphist of "In the Cage," he observes, "The two little spirits of maidens, in the group, bear up, oddly enough, beyond those of their brothers." [20] For James perspicacious little girls are

19. Henry James, *The Art of the Novel*, ed. R. P. Blackmur (New York, 1934), pp. 143–44.
20. Ibid., p. 156.

tougher than perspicacious little boys, and it is partly for this reason that he was more concerned with their education than with that of their brothers. Pansy Osmond is the first sketch of what was in 1899 to become the finished portrait of the Jamesian *jeune fille*. The adolescent's gift of perception has yet to be tempered with strength of character and a moral sense. James's *jeune fille* had some distance to go before she would emerge in a successful synthesis of the old and new ways of educating the young.

CHAPTER VII

Maisie

Maisie Farange, of *What Maisie Knew* (1897), is the logical consequence of James's growing interest in the child as reflector of complex thought and feeling.[1] In "The Pupil," the author still felt the need of an intervening consciousness to interpret and comment on Morgan. With *Maisie* the potential of the child as central intelligence is completely developed and the novelist's educational philosophy is fully articulated. James's notebook entries of this period are numerous and specific. His detailed discussion of *Maisie* testifies to the depth of his involvement with the work in terms of method and theme.

James first recorded the idea for the story of a child of divorced parents on November 12, 1892. He instantly saw the dramatic possibilities in a situation that would produce "suspicion, jealousy . . . with the innocent child in the midst." On August 26, 1893, the "subject of the *partagé* child—of divorced parents" began to take form. It was not, however, until December 22, 1895, that the novelist recorded his decision to use the child's point of view exclusively: "Make my point of view, my *line*, the consciousness, the dim, sweet, scared, wondering, clinging perception of the child, and one gets something like *this*." [2]

The rest of the lengthy and detailed entry is devoted to an outline of the plot for the novel. James had started out

1. Henry James, *What Maisie Knew* (New York, 1954). This edition, rather than the New York Edition, is used for references in this chapter.
2. *The Notebooks of Henry James*, ed. F. O. Matthiessen and Kenneth B. Murdock (New York, 1962), p. 236.

to achieve ironic interest by making Maisie a pawn of parents who "transmit the little girl to the persons they each have married *en secondes noces*." [3] As he expands on the original idea, the child takes on another dimension. She becomes, even as James conjectures about possible situations in which to place her, more directly involved with, and affected by, her experience. Crucial scenes begin to take place "before Maisie—everything takes place before Maisie." [4] The child's exposure becomes her education. As "the child's perceptions of the situation at first—its wonderings, bewilderment, then gradual clever little perception of what it must do" [5] crystallized for James; her developing awareness becomes a protective armor against the thoughtless cruelty of the adult world. It is noteworthy that James changed the name he had originally assigned to Maisie's family. The Hurters of the 1893 entry became the Faranges in 1895. It is possible that more than the desire to avoid a too descriptive name motivated the change. As Maisie becomes more aware, she becomes less vulnerable to the "hurt" that her irresponsible parents inflict upon her. Like Dolcino, Morgan, Effie, and Miles, she will be sacrificed on the altar of adult egotism; unlike them, she will emerge unscathed. The sacrifice brings regeneration to those around her, not by her death, however, but by the "death of her childhood"—by the achievement of maturity. Maisie lives and takes part in shaping her own destiny as well as those of the adults who come in contact with her. James changed his conception of the child as he was in the process of fashioning her from passive victim to "a more or less active conscious agent achieving a 'better state' for herself." [6] James's final notebook discussion of his plan for *What Maisie Knew* is dated October 26, 1896, and is devoted mainly to working out the technical problems connected with the effective dramati-

3. Ibid., p. 134.
4. Ibid., p. 238.
5. Ibid., p. 236.
6. Ward S. Worden, "Henry James's *What Maisie Knew:* A Comparison with the Plans in *The Notebooks*," *PMLA*, LXVIII (June, 1953), 372.

zation of forces that shape Maisie's character. The care
James lavished on his method (as reflected in this entry)
indicates how eager he was to render the sensibility of
the girl-child in all its nuances.

There was never a time in the memory of this little girl
when her parents were not divorced, when she was not
bounced back and forth between them like "a little
feathered shuttlecock." "Everything that had happened
when she was really little was dormant, everything but
the positive certitude, bequeathed from afar by [her
first governess], that the natural way for a child to have
her parents was separate and successive, like her mutton
and her pudding or her bath and her nap." (*Maisie*, p. 29)

The situation in which the helpless child finds herself
is precarious enough; in addition, her parents ruthlessly
and destructively use her to feed their mutual hate. The
sacrifice of little Dolcino (or of Effie) is largely an unconscious act on the part of the adults involved; the
anger is hidden behind diverse subterfuges. Maisie's parents make no attempt to disguise their attitude toward
her: "They wanted her not for any good they could do
her, but for the harm they could, with her unconscious
aid, do each other. She should serve their anger and seal
their revenge, for husband and wife had been alike crip-
pled by the heavy hand of justice, which in the last resort
met on neither side their indignant claim to get, as they
called it, everything." (*Maisie*, p. 19)

Maisie is "a ready vessel for bitterness, a deep little
porcelain cup in which biting acids could be mixed." What
is more, she is "used" by all the adults who come in
contact with her. A nameless distant relative does appear
fleetingly at the beginning of the novel and offers to
take Maisie off her mother's hands; she is the only character who is aware of the relevance of the child's emotional environment to her spiritual and intellectual
growth. That "good lady" is unique in her appreciation of
the fate that awaits a little girl caught in the cross-
currents of her parents' aggressive feelings for each other:
"Her silence was a grim judgement of the whole point of
view. 'Poor little monkey!' she at last exclaimed; and the

words were an epitaph for the tomb of Maisie's childhood. She was abandoned to her fate." (*Maisie*, p. 19)

Aside from this sensitive woman, no one—and this includes the people who are kind to her as well as those who are cruel—sees in Maisie anything other than a means by which they can further their own ends. For Miss Overmore, the governess who becomes her stepmother, she is at first "a little duenna" who makes possible a relationship with the child's father. After Miss Overmore's marriage to Beale and Sir Claude's marriage to Ida, the child is used by both step-parents to advance their illicit romance. Even faithful old Mrs. Wix, her final governess, uses Maisie as a substitute for her own "little dead Clara Matilda" and as bait to convince Sir Claude to stay with them rather than go off with Mrs. Beale. In *What Maisie Knew* James speaks clearly through the consciousness of the child against the inhumanity of the egotistical adult world.

Ida and Beale Farange belong, as do Mrs. Beale and Sir Claude, to "a society in which for the most part people were occupied only with chatter . . . everybody was always assuring everybody of something very shocking, and nobody would have been jolly if nobody had been outrageous." It is a superficial, amoral, irresponsible world that James condemns and was to depict with greater subtlety and equally vigorous censure in *The Awkward Age*.

Maisie is irresponsibly relegated to the care of a series of governesses engaged for reasons that have little to do with their qualifications as teachers and guardians of the young. Moddle, her first governess, is a foolish, unfeeling woman who is "terribly truthful" about Maisie's spindly legs and the precariousness of her position as a child of divorced parents. What she says to the little girl does not in the least concern Beale as long as she does not interfere with the important business of communicating his hatred to his former wife through the child. When Moddle objects to the message Beale sends to Ida via the four-year-old Maisie—"He said I was to tell you, from him . . . that you're a nasty horrid pig!"—she is whisked from the child's life. Miss Overmore is engaged by Ida because "she's a lady and yet awfully poor," the fact of her superior breeding being demonstrated by the way she crooked her finger at tea. The same young governess is retained by Beale because she is sexually attractive and obviously available for employment that has no connection with the nursery. Mrs. Wix, in her little ugly snuff-colored dress, with her "straighteners" and her complete ignorance in matters of the schoolroom, is gotten "for such low pay, really for nothing."

Maisie's numerous mothers and fathers make no attempt to create even an illusion of respectability. A succession of her mother's lovers—before and after her marriage to Sir Claude—pass before the child's eyes as if this performance were a homely characteristic of family life. Mr. Perrimen, Lord Eric, and the Captain are as much a part of Maisie's experience as the games Sir Claude provides for her which she cannot quite understand how to play. Ida's irresponsibility in sexual matters is paralleled by Beale's, and Sir Claude's subsequent love affair with Mrs. Beale completes the child's vision of a world in which fidelity, integrity, and loyalty do not exist between men and women, a world in which marriage is synonymous with duplicity and unaccountability.

The people who figure prominently in Maisie's life, whose behavior impinges directly on the consciousness of the little girl, are depicted as varying in degree of complexity; they emerge, in the main, as emblematic of the multiform aspects of societal as well as parental failure. Least complicated is Ida Farange, Maisie's mother, who is more of an ominous presence permeating the atmosphere of the novel than a fully rendered character; she seldom appears, but her personality dominates throughout. She is always there, just behind the scenes, ready to attack. The range of emotion that she exhibits is small. She is either intensely irritable or uncontrolledly angry; in either case, Maisie is the direct or indirect target of her hostility. Her irritation with the little girl begins early, when the child instinctively refuses to serve her vengeful needs by becoming a silent and passive observer of the battle raging between her parents:

> "It doesn't in the least matter, you know, what you think," Mrs. Farange loudly replied; "and you had better indeed for future, miss, learn to keep your thoughts to yourself." This was exactly what Maisie had already learned, and the accomplishment was just the source of her mother's irritation. (*Maisie*, p. 31)

If she is monotonous in her monstrosity, she is so conceived as to effectively sound the note of hate that James envisioned as the most destructive force Maisie had to meet and overcome. Ida is most completely rendered in the scene, toward the end of the novel, when she comes to Folkestone to rid herself of the child forever. James presents her as a kind of inhuman, disembodied aggregate of "high fair drapery," "stiff sheen," and honeyed words, beneath the surface of which the ultimate rejection a child can suffer lies waiting to show itself in its unmistakable clarity and unspeakable heartlessness. For the first time in the novel Ida speaks "in a tone that enriched the whole surprise by its unexpected softness" because she is determined to finally and irrevocably be free of the burden of the child. Maisie senses this from the first: "She had the positive sense of their catching their relative, catching her in the act of getting rid of her burden with a finality that showed her as unprecedentedly relaxed. Oh yes, the fear had dropped, and she had never been so irrevocably parted with as in the pressure of possession now supremely exerted by Ida's long-gloved and much bangled arm." (*Maisie*, p. 169) In spite of her perception of her mother's motive, Maisie is so starved for warmth and affection that she is grateful for even this perverted manifestation of maternal feeling. The child becomes aware of Ida's vivid beauty, her charm, the source of her attraction to men, and she responds to it with honest appreciation. Thus James makes Ida more real for the reader and her abandonment of Maisie more moving. The scene in which Ida slowly, falteringly but determinedly seeks to disengage herself from the child is deeply touching. The child knows from the start that her mother wants to be rid of her, and she has only one concern; Maisie wants their parting to take place on this rare note of kindness and warmth that her mother is sounding for the first time in her relations with the little girl:

It was really the occasion of Maisie's life on which her mother was to have most to say to her. . . . All her interviews, all her ordeals with her mother had, as she had grown older, seemed to have . . . the hard quality of duration; but longer than any, strangely, were these minutes offered her as so pacific and so agreeably winding up the connexion. It was her anxiety that made them long, her fear of some hitch, some check of the current. . . . She held her breath; she only wanted, by playing into her visitor's hands, to see the thing through. (*Maisie*, p. 175 and p. 177)

The poor child's apprehension is justified. She speaks at the wrong moment—unfortunately just as Ida is to make the grand gesture of giving the child money—and of the wrong person, the Captain, who has by this time become one of Ida's discarded lovers. The spell is broken and Ida reverts to her more familiar self. Her parting words to her daughter are "You're a dreadful dismal deplorable little thing." James's portrait of Ida Farange is consistent and complete just as Maisie's perception of her was accurate.

Beale Farange, with "his vast fair beard, burnished like a gold breast-plate" and his glittering teeth "that his long moustache had been trained not to hide," is not as directly destructive as his wife. If she infuses the novel with an atmosphere of hate, he imbues it with an air of irresponsibility. Rarely angry or irritable, he just does not care, and his lack of concern is usually covered by a boisterous good humor. His most despicable acts have an air of jollity about them: "[Maisie's] first term was with her father, who spared her only in not letting her have the wild letters addressed to her by her mother: he confined himself to holding them up at her and shaking them, while he showed his teeth, and then amusing her by the way he chucked them, across the room, bang into the fire." (*Maisie*, pp. 23–24) The rowdy, cigarette-

smoking gentlemen visitors who pull and pinch and tease
her about her abnormally thin legs; the "friendly noisy
little house"; her papa's tendency to "burst into one of
those loud laughs of his that, however prepared she was,
seemed always, like some trick in a frightening game,
to leap forth and make her jump"—all this has a surface conviviality that obscures a disregard for the child.
Like Ida, Beale does not appear very often; they are
absentee parents. When he does appear, he is seen obliquely through Mrs. Beale's observations about him, a
way of stressing his uninvolvement. Beale Farange is the
embodiment of wanton unaccountability in human relations, a kind of behavior Maisie will learn to recognize
and repudiate.

Ida's final rejection of her daughter is paralleled in the
scene when Beale whisks Maisie away from the Exhibition
to the home of his rich mistress, the Countess. Like Ida,
his aim is to unburden himself of the child, but what
transpires between Maisie and Beale has a different tonal
quality than the scene at Folkestone and is thoroughly
consistent with the particular aspect of parental dereliction which James is emphasizing: "Beale Farange stood
and smiled at his young lady, his back to the fanciful
fireplace, his light overcoat—the very lightest in London—
wide open, and his wonderful lustrous beard completely
concealing the expanse of shirt-front. It pleased her more
than ever to think that papa was handsome and, though
as high aloft as mamma and almost, in his specially florid
evening dress, as splendid, of a beauty somehow less
belligerent, less terrible." (*Maisie*, p. 146)

And poor little Maisie is, for the moment, lulled into a
false sense of being loved and wanted. Beale's charm is
so much easier to respond to than her mother's; her
habitually keen intuitive faculty is dulled by the emotions
of the moment: ". . . there was an increasing sweetness
for his daughter in being with him so long without his
doing anything worse. The whole hour of course was to
remain with her, for days and weeks, ineffaceably illu-
mined and confirmed; by the end of which she was able
to read into it a hundred things that had been at the

moment mere miraculous pleasantries." (*Maisie*, p. 147)
Beale's "foolish tenderness," his playful affection and the
"fragrance of his cherished beard" cannot, for long, obscure the depth of his egotism. Indeed he might be considered more culpable than his wife; his seeming tenderness and concern render his abandonment of Maisie more
cruelly shocking to her:

> Wasn't he trying to turn the table on her, embarrass her some-
> how into admitting that what would really suit her little book
> would be, after doing so much for good manners, to leave her
> wholly at liberty to arrange for herself? . . . it rolled over her
> that this was their parting, their parting forever, and that he
> had brought her there for so many caresses only because it
> was important such an occasion should look better for him
> than any other. . . . Then she understood as well as if he had
> spoken it that what he wanted, hang it, was that she should
> let him off with all the honours . . . with all the appearance of
> virtue and sacrifice on his side. (*Maisie*, p. 153)

Beale forces Maisie to shoulder the responsibility of his
abandonment of her. She must "repudiate her dear old
daddy—in the face, mind you, of his tender supplica-
tions," thus absorbing the guilt of his malefaction.
Maisie's mother calls her a monster through clenched
teeth; her father does it through a roar of laughter.

Mrs. Beale, Maisie's step-mother, is less reprehensible
because her obligation to the child is less compelling. Accordingly James has presented her as more frivolous than
unkind, emblematic of yet another kind of delinquency.
Mrs. Beale is careless in her relations with people and her
thoughtless egotism derives from her unbridled impulse
to satisfy her sensual needs. Her response to Maisie's
papa, "smiling and flashing his beautiful teeth at [me]
the time we met him in the Park" is scarcely different
from her later reaction to Sir Claude—"He keeps me up
splendidly he does. . . ." Both responses are primitive
in that they do not reflect any consideration beyond the
gratification of the immediate need. Mrs. Beale truly
cannot understand why Sir Claude is reluctant to involve
Maisie in their illicit relationship:

> "He says he doesn't want you mixed up."
> "Mixed up with what?" [asks Maisie]

"That's exactly what *I* want to know: mixed up with what—
and how you are any more mixed—?" Mrs. Beale paused without ending her question. She ended after an instant in a different way. "All you can say is that it's his fancy." (*Maisie*,
pp. 139–40)

Mrs. Beale is neither vicious nor hateful, just completely
and unconsciously (even good naturedly) amoral. Actually, she is rather fond of Maisie, in the same way that
she is fond of all who gratify her needs; once they refuse
to feed her selfishness, she simply loses interest in them.
She too eventually calls Maisie a "little horror," but it is
more in frustration than in anger when she senses the
possibility of denial in Sir Claude's wavering moral prin-
ciples:

"*Will* you give him up?" Maisie persisted to Mrs. Beale.
"To *you*, you abominable little horror?" that lady in-
dignantly inquired. . . . Have you been a hideous little hypo-
crite all these years that I've slaved to make you love me and
deludedly believed you did?" (*Maisie*, p. 277)

Mrs. Beale's effort to keep Maisie with her and Sir Claude
stems from a selfish need for a semblance of respectability and the desire to secure the tie with Maisie's step-
father. Mindless self-interest lies behind her desperate
appeal to the child. Maisie recognizes her step-mother's
frivolity, her lack of comprehension of what constitutes
responsible behavior. Mrs. Beale's parting words to
Maisie illuminate the disparity between the worlds they
inhabit:

Mrs. Beale . . . faced full at Maisie. "I don't know what to
make of you!" . . . "Good-bye!" she hurled at Maisie; then
passed straight across the room and disappeared in the ad-
joining one. (*Maisie*, p. 279)

More complex is James's portrait of Sir Claude, Maisie's
beloved step-father and the hero-manqué of the novel.
For all his virtues (and there are many) he fails Maisie
at the crucial moment. He truly cares for Maisie—but not
enough to transcend his weakness. He is prepared to
shoulder the responsibility of the child—but not at the
expense of denying himself his sexual indulgence. Like
Mrs. Beale, Sir Claude is a slave to his sensuality; unlike

her, he has a sense of decency that complicates yet, strangely enough, simplifies life for him. His moral sense comes into direct conflict with his appetite; this makes decisive action difficult for him, but it simultaneously provides him with a realistic view of his situation and ultimately with the strength needed to help Maisie make the right choice. Through Sir Claude, James is saying that feeling and perception are, in the final analysis, not enough to make a complete human being; true virtue must include self-discipline and the strength to reject momentary satisfaction. Maisie has the will that Sir Claude lacks and he is aware of his deficiency: "It wouldn't do," he says to Mrs. Beale. "'We *can't* work her in. It's perfectly true—she's unique. We're not good enough—oh no!' and quite exuberantly, he laughed again." (*Maisie*, p. 278) The pleasure that Sir Claude feels at the moment of self-recognition derives from his feeling of relief at being permitted, after all, to pursue his life of self-indulgence. His perception of Maisie's strength and his acceptance of his own weakness resolves his conflict for him. He is not called upon to shoulder responsibility or make choices; in short, he need not become a complete person; Maisie has done it for him. The reversal of roles that James has implied throughout the novel—Maisie as judge of those who should judge and as guide to those who should guide—is fully realized in Sir Claude's repudiation of maturity and Maisie's acceptance of it.

By the time Maisie is called upon to choose between her step-parents and Mrs. Wix, she has evolved into a self-contained, mature little person. Her growing awareness through the course of the novel has enabled her to differentiate between ephemeral and constant values. But, like all sentient people, Maisie must feel truly needed in order to be complete within herself. This is the function of Mrs. Wix—to give Maisie the feeling that her existence is of consequence to someone. The little old governess is shabby, ugly, ignorant, and, to a certain degree, self-seeking, but she needs Maisie to give meaning to her own life, and the child feels it at her first encounter with the woman. Unlike the manipulative attempts of other adults, Mrs. Wix's effort to "use" the little girl is inextricably bound up with her readiness to give of herself in return: "[Mrs. Wix] had struck her at first, just after Miss Overmore, as terrible; but something in her voice at the end of an hour touched the little girl in a spot that had never yet been reached. Maisie knew later what it was. . . . What Maisie felt was that she had been with passion and anguish, a mother, and that this was something Miss Overmore was not, something (strangely, confusingly) that mama was even less." (*Maisie*, p. 34)

Mrs. Wix is in every way the direct antithesis of Ida Farange and, as such, she becomes the embodiment of the mother-figure for Maisie, one who radiates feelings traditionally associated with motherhood—kindness, fidelity, concern. Through Mrs. Wix, James is commenting on a society in which these qualities have become irrelevant. In the "new" world of high fashion, promiscuity and chatter represented by the Faranges and their subsequent spouses, conscience and decency are considered old and dingy relics of a shabby world. In choosing to go with Mrs. Wix, Maisie is rejecting this "new" dehumanized world. Maisie does not need Mrs. Wix as moral guardian, the proportions of the child's moral sense being so much greater and on much more solid ground than that of the old governess. What she responds to in Mrs. Wix is the woman's need for someone to live for, her eagerness to give in return the love, warmth, and acceptance Maisie has never known. Mrs. Wix is far from the ideal parental figure for Maisie, whose intelligence, perception, and judgement so far exceed her own; but James told us that Maisie was destined to lend "to poorer persons and things, by the mere fact of their being involved with her and by the special scale she creates for them, a precious element of dignity." [7] Thus Maisie is left with the problem of Mrs. Wix's education; the redeeming feature of this reversal of roles is the knowledge that the poor old governess will appreciate Maisie's tutelage and repay it with what is essentially the foundation

7. Henry James, *The Art of the Novel*, ed. R. P. Blackmur (New York, 1934), p. 147.

of familial relations—unquestioning affection. In the dark world of Maisie Farange, that is quite a lot.

In view of James's detailed notebook entries, his comprehensive preface in his New York Edition, and indeed in view of the novel itself, some of the critical pronouncements on *What Maisie Knew* have been surprising. The novel, and more specifically its heroine, has occasioned such a variety of explications that one is often tempted to analyze the critics rather than the character. One commentator suggests that the juvenile Maisie's response to Sir Claude is purely sexual, that she is prepared to offer her virginity in order to win him from Mrs. Beale,[8] a notion that would, one suspects, have astonished the author of the novel. For another Maisie is "a combination of purity and corruption" having her own "subtly distinct moral coloration."[9] Yet another finds *Maisie* a "high-spirited comedy."[10] A fifth expositor insists that Maisie's ego emerges at the end as "untrained, unsustained, ill-formed, and ethically illiterate, an ego that will satisfy itself even at the cost of what it regards as everything."[11] The presumption in this last comment is that James had no idea what he was doing, that the work is an aggregate of its author's unconscious drives, an approach that does little to illuminate any work of art. *What Maisie Knew*, like James's best fiction, has an illusive quality and its fair share of ambiguity. His strength as a novelist lies, in no small measure, in his ability to engage the imaginative faculty of the reader, to stimulate him to recreate the characters, to some degree, in his own image. But James was a self-conscious and disciplined artist; his work should be judged on how well it accomplishes its manifest purpose.

For the most part, however, critics have tended to view

8. Harris W. Wilson, "What *Did* Maisie Know?" *College English,* XVII (February, 1956), 279–82.

9. Edward W. Wasiolek, "Maisie: Pure or Corrupt?" *College English,* XXII (December, 1960), 169–72.

10. F. R. Leavis, "James's *What Maisie Knew:* A Disagreement," *Scrutiny,* XVII (Summer, 1950), 119.

11. John C. McCloskey, "What Maisie Knows: A Study of Childhood and Adolescence," *American Literature,* 36 (January, 1965), 513.

Maisie within the context of James's obvious intent—as the chronicle of a child's struggle to transcend the evil of which she is unwittingly a part, and of her intellectual and moral growth during the process. More recent critical comment has tended to emphasize Maisie's relevance to a world from which a clearly defined value system has all but disappeared. James's theme of the ironic reversal of roles is timeless and universal; it has particular significance, however, in an era of confusion and aimlessness such as our own. The disordered world of Maisie offers a striking parallel to contemporary society and her quest for identity dramatizes a modern dilemma.

It seems to me, however, that the tendency to subsume the character of Maisie in the theme of moral superiority stems in part from an attempt by critics to reconcile James's rendering of Maisie with the concept of what a child in her position would *really* be like. Maisie is not, nor was she meant to be, the documented case-history of a product of divorce; she is essentially a typical Jamesian heroine, albeit a child, supremely intelligent in the midst of gross stupidity, innocently pure in the midst of miry corruption, and ultimately victorious in the face of seeming defeat. What differentiates James's treatment of Maisie from that of his adult heroines is his authoritative documentation of her perceptions which is rooted in his understanding of and empathy for the child's sensibility. James knew—or perhaps he remembered—precisely how the world could look to a young child, how experience impinged upon the consciousness of the young, and he projected this faithfully in his rendering of Maisie:

. . . [Maisie] found in her mind a collection of images and echoes to which meanings were attachable—images and echoes kept for her in the childish dusk, the dim closet, the high drawers, like games she wasn't yet big enough to play. The great strain meanwhile was that of carrying by the right end the things her father said about her mother—things mostly indeed that [her governess], on a glimpse of them, as if they had been complicated toys or difficult books, took out of her hands and put away in the closet. A wonderful assortment of objects of this kind she was to discover there later, all tumbled up too with the things, shuffled into some receptacle, that her mother had said about her father. (*Maisie*, p. 25)

This recreation of the repressive mechanism at work in terms of images that are salient for a child is characteristic of James's sensitive grasp of the child's response to external stimuli. The moment of Maisie's initiation into total awareness of her function for her parents is recorded with chilling lucidity: "The theory of her stupidity, eventually embraced by her parents, corresponded with a great date in her small still life: the complete vision, private but final, of the strange office she filled. It was literally a moral revolution and accomplished in the depths of her nature . . . old forms and phrases began to have a sense that frightened her. She had a new feeling, the feeling of danger: on which a new remedy rose to meet it, the idea of an inner self or, in other words, of concealment." (*Maisie*, p. 27)

The little girl's recoil from hostility and rejection is authentically documented. James goes on to identify the weapon the young sensibility will forge in order to protect itself: "She would forget everything, she would repeat nothing, and when, as a tribute to the successful application of her system, she began to be called a little idiot, she tasted a pleasure new and keen. . . . She spoiled their fun, but she practically added to her own. She saw more and more; she saw too much." (*Maisie*, p. 28)

James's handling of Maisie's early development has a psychological verisimilitude that is almost painful in its accuracy. Young Maisie "had come to like people's liking her to 'know.' " She learns that "sometimes patient little silences and intelligent little looks could be rewarded by delightful little glimpses." On one of the few occasions when James shifts from Maisie's point of view to that of the omniscient author, it is to comment on the destructive nature of Maisie's defensive "voyeurism": ". . . while [Beale and Maisie] sat together, there was an extraordinary mute passage between her vision of this vision of his, his vision of her vision, and her vision of his vision of her vision. What there was no effective record of indeed was the small strange pathos on the child's part of an innocence so saturated with knowledge and so directed to diplomacy." (*Maisie*, p. 150)

In spite of James's carefully delineated record of Maisie's reactions to her experiences, there is an essential element missing in his projection of her; this omission furthers the development of the author's theme but it robs Maisie of psychological authenticity. Despite the brutality to which the child is exposed, she is completely devoid of anger or resentment. Because Maisie bears no grudges, her moral sense is free to develop to its fullest capacity. But the little girl's lack of anger, in view of the emotional laceration her life experience must have given her, is difficult to accept. Critics have tried to avoid the problem by pointing out the especial nature of the child's intuitive faculty or the redemptive quality of Mrs. Wix's devotion. But Mrs. Wix's undeniable warmth is not enough to neutralize feelings of rejection instilled in early childhood:

She was familiar, at the age of six, with the fact that everything had been changed on her account . . . she was to remember always the words in which Moddle impressed upon her that her father did so give himself: "Your papa wishes you never to forget, you know, that he has been dreadfully put about." (*Maisie*, p. 25)

What compensation can there be for a child who is told by her father, "You know your mother loathes you, loathes you simply." Who can ever erase from the child's memory the words "Your father wishes you were dead— that, my dear, is what your father wishes. You'll have to get used to it as I have done—I mean his wishing that *I'm* dead." There is a limit to the amount of hate a child can absorb without having some of it rub off on her own little person. While James dealt magnificently with causes in his presentation of the child's character and plight, he has not adequately dramatized effects. What Maisie comes to know does not—if we are to think of her in terms of psychological realism—affect her in ways the reader can accept. In his preface to the 1907 edition James states that he was not aiming at psychological verisimilitude in his portrait of Maisie: "For satisfaction of the mind . . . the small expanding consciousness would have to be saved, have to become presentable as a register of impressions; and saved by the experience of certain advantage . . . rather than coarsened, blurred, sterilized, by ignorance and pain. . . ." [12]

Maisie thus becomes the embodiment of a wish-fulfillment dream, a kind of Horatio Alger of the mental and spiritual life, an emotional "success story." With *What Maisie Knew* a new and different abused Jamesian child appeared, one who "flourish[ed] to a degree, at the cost of many conventions and proprieties, even decencies, really keeping the torch of virtue alive in an air tending infinitely to smother it; really in short making confusion worse confounded by drawing some stray fragrance of an ideal across the scent of selfishness, by sowing barren strands, through the mere fact of presence, the seed of the moral life." [13]

There are essentially three ways in which a young child can deal with the inevitable anger provoked by rejection. It might turn these feelings inward, and the result would be some form of self-destruction; these feelings could be projected outward, and the result could be a destructive impulse toward society; a third alternative lies in the sublimation of this hostile energy into socially sanctioned activity. For Maisie, none of these alternatives exists. The achievement of a state of moral superiority is a result of successful sublimation, not a substitute for it. The development of Maisie's moral sense does not correlate with her emotional development; in terms of realistic portraiture, one could not conceivably run parallel to the other. While James exhibits psychological discernment in his rendering of Maisie's perception of the world, he fails to face the implications of those perceptions for the child. In Maisie, James has created what was perhaps for him the ideal child, one that is victimized and aware, yet free from aggression and hostility, one who "live[s] with all intensity and perplexity in its terribly mixed little world," but who could, one suspects, only exist in the world of James's rich and creative imagination. But to leave it at that would be to

12. James, *The Art of the Novel*, p. 142.
13. Ibid., p. 143.

ignore the work of art. The rare quality of the novel lies in the delicacy of response on the part of the novelist to the movement of the child's mind, in the figurative language that so sensitively captures the pain of childhood and growing up, and in the author's sustained metaphoric use of the child as a force for spiritual health and moral superiority. In a sense, we all share James's dream of emancipation from our baser feelings; it is the novelist's consummate skill in his realization of her that endears Maisie to us. If he has not fully succeeded in bodying forth a psychologically complete figure in his child-heroine, he has given an authentic picture of what the world can look like to a sensitive little girl and, through her perceptions, a sense of the latent ugliness of life. In *What Maisie Knew* the author focused on a more terrible cruelty that can be perpetrated on children—the cruelty of subjecting them to chaos and confusion as well as emotional deprivation. Love and order (says James through Maisie) are closely related in the child's world. Affection cannot exist without a coherent value system; both are indispensable for the well-being of the young. Maisie's anguished plea to the Captain to love her mother not "just for a little but for always" is the first of a new, a modern "cry of the children." It is a plea for love, acceptance, and the order of continuity—the cry that gives the twentieth-century characterization of children in fiction its unique tone.

CHAPTER VIII

The Maturing Process

With Maisie, James achieved his most completely realized representation of a small child's sensibility. It was his one novel-length exploration of the consciousness of a young female child. In subsequent works the novelist was to focus on adolescence and the problems of maturation. James's interest in the theme predates by almost three decades his preoccupation with it in the 1890's. For the genesis of his concern with this motif we must look back to his earliest novel. *Watch and Ward* was written in 1870, when the author was twenty-eight years old; it was serialized in the *Atlantic Monthly*, August–December, 1871, and published in novel form (after extensive revision) in 1878.[1] Records show that James revised the work largely to protect his copyright and to give the novel a more finished appearance in the light of his maturing reputation; there were also financial considerations. Changes that he made in the text reflect an effort to achieve precision and simplicity. He did not alter the "story-line."

The novel remains a curious tale of a young New England bachelor who adopts a twelve-year-old girl, supervises her education, and decides early that she will grow up to be an ideal wife for him. The reader is immediately struck by the quality of the writing, which is embarrassingly naïve in its projection of certain erotic elements. Unless he writes tongue in cheek, the young novelist could not possibly have been aware of the implications of his hero's day-dream about the young girl he has adopted: ". . . in his desire to order all things well, Roger caught himself wondering whether, at the

1. Henry James, *Watch and Ward* (New York, 1960).

worst, a little precursory love-making would do any harm. The ground might be gently tickled to receive his own sowing; the petals of the young girl's nature, playfully forced apart, would leave the golden heart of the flower but the more accessible to his own vertical rays." (*Watch and Ward*, p. 81)

The novel contains several such passages suggesting that its young author expressed libidinal feelings—seemingly without awareness—through the fantasies of his hero. The fledgling novelist's predilection for the melodramatic as well as his tendency to emphasize external action at the expense of character development is very much in evidence in this first novel. For the student of Henry James, *Watch and Ward* is of singular interest. The novel is a rich source of themes to be elaborated upon and characters to be developed in later works. In his introduction to the 1960 edition of the novel, Leon Edel shows how its themes and characters were to appear in such finished works as *The Portrait of a Lady*, *The Wings of the Dove, Washington Square*, and *The Awkward Age*. The novel itself, unfortunately, has little relevance beyond the historical; its old-fashioned charm hardly compensates for technical deficiencies. The child, Nora Lambert, is not convincing. Little girls do not "wring [their] hands" nor do they ordinarily "rush into [the] embrace" of strange men. Yet there are passages that demonstrate the young author's understanding of a child's physical and emotional needs: "She grew more hardy and lively, more inquisitive, more active. She tasted deeply of the joy of tattered dresses and sun-burnt cheeks and arms, and long nights at the end of tired days." (*Watch and Ward*, p. 50)

Such insight is rare, however, perhaps because James was less interested in Nora's childhood experience than in her possibilities as an object of romantic interest. She is seen from the first in terms of the woman she is to become. "He leaned back in his chair and looked at the child,—the little forlorn, precocious, potential woman." Roger Lawrence's response to her is never as an adult to a child; there are always overtones of the man-woman

relationship. This is apparent from the moment Roger
first meets the child after her father's suicide. " 'Do you
remember my taking you last night in my arms?' [he asks
the child the morning after the tragedy]. It was his fancy
that, for answer, she faintly blushed." And again, "He
put his arm round her waist. An irrestible sense of her
childish sweetness, of her tender feminine promise, stole
softly into his pulses." The young bachelor's feeling for
the child could hardly be characterized as paternal. Roger
sees her immediately as a "poor little uprooted germ of
womanhood." Nora is only incidentally a child and Roger
extrinsically a father figure. Yet there is undeniable evidence in this first novel of James's interest in the process
of growth. The young novelist is already articulating his
principle of awareness as a prior condition for healthy
development. "He perceived at last . . . that her listless
quietude covered a great deal of observation, and that
growing may be a very soundless process." And the seeds
of the Jamesian fine consciousness are evident in her
"instinct to have perceived the fitness of not speaking of
her own affairs" and her "precocious good taste."

While Nora prefigures the observant and intuitively
perceptive child of James's mature work, there is little
evidence in this early novel of a specific or unique educative philosophy; for young James education was still
a matter of grammar, catechism, and limited intellectual
curiosity—"Might she not (horror of horrors!) turn out
too clever?" Increasingly maturity was to become, for
James, a matter of intrinsic attributes—perception, a
fine sensibility, an intuitive morality. Less and less was
it to be contingent upon externals—formal training, material well-being, parental example. At this phase of his
development, however, he expressed the conventional
view of his day. Excessive awareness was something to
be shunned in the young and the acquisition of knowledge a matter of externally imposed conditions: "He determined . . . to lay the smooth foundation-stones of
Nora's culture, to teach her to read and write and ci-
pher, to associate himself largely with the growth of her
primal sense of things." (*Watch and Ward*, p. 43)

Yet Roger, in his role of father, is in no small measure a projection of the ideal parent, the antithesis to such scathing examples of parental dereliction as the Moreens, the Faranges, and the Brookenhams who were to people James's later works. Roger's motives may be questionable but his behavior to the child is exemplary:

> Roger began also to anticipate the future exactions of preceptorship. He plunged into a course of useful reading, and devoured a hundred volumes on education, on hygiene, on morals, on history. He drew up a table of rules and observances for the child's health; he weighed and measured her food, and spent hours with [the housekeeper], the minister's wife, and the doctor, in the discussion of her regimen and clothing. He bought her a pony, and rode with her over the neighbouring county, roamed with her in the woods and fields, and picked out nice acquaintances for her among the little damsels of the countryside. . . . He passed a dozen times a week from the fear of coddling and spoiling the child to the fear of letting her run wild and grow coarse and rustic. (*Watch and Ward*, p. 43)

For James there was clearly no substitute for parental concern and devotion. This early work states explicitly that fundamental to the educative process is a lively intelligence in the learner and an earnest commitment in the parental guide. *Watch and Ward* augurs James's lifelong dedication to this principle.

James never wavered in his allegiance to this ideal and by the time he created his finished tales about adolescents, he had arrived at a clearly defined concept of what constituted maturity. He is concerned in the tales of the 1890's with defining attributes of character and personality that will ensure maximal spiritual and emotional growth. Familial relations always were, and continued to be, fundamental determinants of character and personality for James, but his emerging adults of this period are notable for the battle they must wage within themselves in order to develop into emotionally sound and morally superior adults. The conflicts they must resolve have an inner focus; they are more intensely personal than public. These young people are poised on the brink of maturity and they are conspicuously energetic in their approach to living. If Pansy, Morgan, and Maisie had their experience of life determined by external circumstances beyond their control, the adolescents who follow actively reach out to life in an effort to understand and shape their destinies. They are markedly curious and they eagerly undertake to examine the difference between illusion and reality, to inquire into the paradox of ambiguity in the face of certainty, and to differentiate between good and evil. These are the questions that James raises and attempts to answer through his emerging adults. For the author "the garden of Youth [was] apt inordinately to bristle." [2] And the literature in which these young people figure is richly connotative in its projection of character, theme, and image. As if to give substance to his notion that "the fact of youth, so far from dispelling ambiguity, positively introduces it," [3] these adolescents of the late 90's are called upon to make some fine distinctions between what is real and unreal, where fact lies and where fiction.

As was the case with his handling of the younger children, there is a progression in James's treatment of the emerging adult; the movement is from unawareness to self-consciousness, from partial insight to complete vision, and from defective perception to full cognition. Like their younger predecessors, James's adolescents become increasingly aware of and responsive to the reality of their life situations; this ability to perceive the truth about oneself and the actuality of one's condition becomes the gauge of the character's moral worth.

The young, inexperienced, and avidly curious governess in "The Turn of the Screw" [4] effectively demonstrates the novelist's interest at this time in the relationship between curiosity and self-knowledge, between certainty and ambiguity. The epistemological and metaphysical motifs that dominate so much of James's fiction were never more fully explored than through his rendering of the young people in "The Turn of the Screw." This is perhaps the most widely known of James's tales. The young

2. Henry James, *The Middle Years* (London, 1917), p. 9.
3. Ibid.
4. Henry James, *The Two Magics* (New York, 1898).

girl, scarcely out of her teens, who accepts the position of governess to two orphaned children on a lonely estate is one of the most ambiguous "heroines" in literature. The children, Flora, aged eight, and Miles, aged ten, have been the subject of as much discussion as their intense little governess. The story of the latter's encounter with the "ghosts"—that of a former governess, Miss Jessel, who died under mysterious circumstances, and that of a servingman, Peter Quint, killed in a mishap on a lonely road near Bly—is well known. The young governess' struggle with these two spirits for "possession" of the innocent children has been successfully adapted to the media of the drama, film, opera, and television. In the academic world the principal narrator of the tale has been the subject of continuing critical controversy. Questions of how much the young governess "sees," whether what she sees is really there, and how subjective her vision might be are crucial to an interpretation of the tale, and the governess has provoked endless discussion on the question of her credibility as narrator. Although many extreme positions have been taken vis-à-vis the governess, no one has remarked that she is a notable, if heightened, portrait of an adolescent. James endowed her with many personality traits that we have come to associate with that difficult period in life when child evolves into adult. Her extremes of sensibility, her passionate dedication to her "cause"—that of "rescuing" the children from evil— her unpredictable changes of mood, and, above all, her insatiable curiosity are all characteristic of the adolescent who is seeking to come to terms with herself and the reality of life. To reduce the governess merely to a "pathological liar" with "an unhinged fancy"[5] robs the tale of its many dimensions. To elevate her to the role of "confessor" and "savior" with a "priestly function"[6] attributes a frame of reference to the author which is questionable in the context of the whole body of his work. The

5. Oscar Cargill, "Henry James as Freudian Pioneer," in *A Casebook of Henry James's "The Turn of the Screw,"* ed. Gerald Willen (New York, 1959), p. 228.
6. Robert Heilman, "The Turn of the Screw as a Poem," in *ibid.*, p. 185.

governess is, to be sure, much more than a typical adolescent; she is the vehicle for James's inquiry into the nature of "seeing" and "knowing," of illusion and reality, of ambiguity and certainty. Yet a measured regard for her adolescent characteristics might very well have tempered the more extreme reactions to her.

The governess' insistence upon knowing all there is to know is a distinctive feature of her personality. This need to know can be viewed as "another form of Faustian pride" [7] or it may be interpreted as a "manifestation of sexual fantasy." [8] It might quite plausibly be seen as "a determination to shape the children's innocence to her own guilt." [9] The source of the governess' compulsion to "know" is subject to discussion; this was, in fact, the author's stated purpose: "It was 'déja très-joli,' in 'The Turn of the Screw,' please believe, the general proposition of our young woman's keeping crystaline her record of so many intense anomalies and obscurities—by which I don't of course mean her explanation of them, a different matter; and I saw no way . . . to exhibit her in relations other than those; one of which, precisely, would have been her relation to her own nature." [10]

But fundamentally the novelist is concerned with the governess' impulse to know and the relationship of that impulse to the attainment of self-knowledge. In a word, is it enough to desperately want knowledge in order to gain it? What are the necessary conditions for "awareness"? Does the governess have a lucid perception of reality? It would seem that, for James, the desire to know does not alone ensure insight. A prior condition for the acquisition of knowledge about others is self-knowledge, which, in turn, implies a recognition of human fallibility. The young governess is sadly deficient in this area. She never sufficiently questions the reality of the "danger"

7. Dorothea Krook, *The Ordeal of Consciousness in Henry James* (Cambridge, England, 1962), p. 126.

8. George Knox, "Incubi and Succubi in *The Turn of the Screw*," *Western Folklore*, XXII (April, 1963), 122.

9. Marius Bewley, *The Complex Fate* (London, 1952), p. 108.

10. Henry James, *The Art of the Novel*, ed. R. P. Blackmur (New York, 1934), pp. 173–74.

she senses: "I saw my service so strongly and so simply. I was there to protect and defend the little creatures in the world the most bereaved and the most lovable . . . we were cut off, really, together; we were united in our danger. . . . I was a screen—I was to stand before them. The more I saw, the less they would." [11]

The governess has but one moment of partial insight —"If he [Miles] were innocent," she cries out at one point, "What then on earth am I?" The implications of the question are too threatening; she dare not pursue it. She might find that what she has attributed to the children is in reality a projection of her own distorted impulse. If the acquisition of knowledge is contingent upon the fullest possible awareness, the governess' one moment of illumination is not enough; part of the horror of the story is precisely this insufficiency in a person responsible for the lives of two children. One need not accept the hypothesis that the governess is "insane" in order to appreciate the precarious position of the children, helpless as they are in the hands of an hysterical guardian.

In order to attain true knowledge one needed the ability to maintain a fine balance between emotion and intellect. The governess' drive to know is emotionally based; it is not tempered by reason and she becomes lost in a labyrinth of her own feelings. Emotion has engulfed cognition to the extent that appearance and reality have become indistinguishable to her—"The more I go over it, the more I see in it, and the more I see in it the more I fear. I don't know what I *don't* see—what I *don't* fear!" The governess lacks the power of discrimination; her mind is rendered as chaotic, cluttered with endless romantic, unrealistic, and even dangerous fantasies. Hers is a nature overwhelmed by emotion; she has lost perspective and cannot understand her own inner turmoil. The fact that James meant her to be viewed in this context is clear from the changes he made in the text in 1907. Every alteration that he made emphasizes the emotional

---

11. James, *The Two Magics*, p. 67. This passage is unrevised in the New York Edition.

aspect of the governess' response to the experience she is recounting.

The *children* do, in fact, "see"—another instance of James's fascination with the theme of the reversal of roles. What the children finally come to "see" is the governess' warped personality. Flora perceives the truth about the governess and, like most of James's little girls, saves herself. " 'Take me away, take me away—oh take me away from *her!*' 'From *me?*' I panted. 'From you— from you!' she cried." As presented, Flora's response to the governess' wild accusation is psychologically sound; it is that of a terrified eight-year-old. Remarkable is the courage with which James has endowed her, the will to escape the horror she senses but cannot define. Flora is, in fact, one of James's transcendent girl-children. Like Pansy Osmond and Maisie Farange before her, she has a firm grip on reality. Like Maisie, too, she has the endurance necessary for self-preservation, the ability to use her insight to advantage. Miles, as well, recognizes that he is caught up in the irrationality of the governess' obsessive drive to "know" at all costs, but like all James's little boys, he does not survive; the horror of his perception frightens him to death.

For James the inability to exercise the cognitive faculty is equated with moral insufficiency. Because the governess does not "see" lucidly and steadily, she is morally deficient. James was ever interested in "the problem of the ethics governing vision." [12] If the character of the adolescent governess seems, at times, overdrawn, it is because James's major interest was in the theme of transition from innocence to knowledge, from adolescence to maturity. Motif took precedence over characterization. The ambiguity with which the author surrounds his narrator is an indispensable part of his projection of the epistemological and metaphysical themes. James's heroine is more emblematic of the stunted adolescent than faithfully representative of the type. And yet, the intense little governess, with her emotional "succession of flights

12. Tony Tanner, *The Reign of Wonder: Naivety and Reality in American Literature* (Cambridge, England, 1965), p. 281.

and drops," her passionate commitment to the "incredibly beautiful" children, her fantasies of how charming it would be "suddenly to meet someone" in the garden at twilight, her unrealistic infatuation with the mysterious and almost unknown guardian of the children, is surprisingly reminiscent of adolescents one has known.

Central to any discussion of James's handling of little Flora and Miles in the tale is the question of the reliability of the narrator-governess. Since all we ever know of the children is what she chooses to reveal about them, the reader is committed to her interpretation of their behavior and her impression of them. Consequently, one of the functions of the children in the tale is to illuminate the state of mind of the governess. Since "The Turn of the Screw" is manifestly a ghostly tale, Flora and Miles serve to intensify the horror that James wished to evoke. This they do in several ways, not the least of which is by the "appalling courage of childhood" they represent.[13] James tells us in his preface that he saw "the haunted children and the prowling servile spirits as a 'value' of the disquieting sort." The idea of innocence habitually associated with childhood would naturally intensify the feeling of recoil at the notion of its corruption. Since the actual moral state of the children is never established, they dramatize the concept of the interrelatedness of good and evil. The governess' perception of them raises the question of the correspondence between appearance and reality, and thus they serve as a touchstone by which the reader may evaluate the governess.

James's "irresponsible little fiction," as he referred to it, must have surpassed his fondest expectations for its success. There appears to be no end to discussions among critics as to whether Flora and Miles are innocent or corrupt; good, evil, or both; symbolically or realistically conceived; and, most controversial of all, whether they do or do not see the ghosts. It is not my intention to review the diverse critical pronouncements on these questions. The controversy and its inconsistencies are documented in

13. Harold C. Goddard, "A Pre-Freudian Reading of *The Turn of the Screw*," *Nineteenth-Century Fiction*, XII (June, 1957), p. 34.

A Casebook on Henry James's "The Turn of the Screw," edited by Gerald Willen, published in 1959, and more recent criticism still centers on these questions.[14] It is my feeling, however, that critics often have tended to view the tale with undue solemnity. An aspect of James frequently overlooked is his sense of fun, and with this facet of his personality in mind, there is no reason to doubt the author's statement of intent in his preface to the tale. ". . . it is a piece of ingenuity pure and simple, of cold artistic calculation, an *amusette* to catch those not easily caught (the 'fun' of the capture of the merely witless being ever but small), the jaded, the disillusioned, the fastidious." The tale is clearly James ultimate exercise in ambiguity. In it he indulges his fascination for the theme of "seeing" and "knowing"; he plays with the question of absolute and relative judgments, and he explores to its fullest possibility the motif of appearance versus reality. The tale exhibits his wry sense of humor and his feeling for the ironic as well as his interest in epistemology.

The children are ingeniously conceived. Whether the reader sees them as the prey of evil spirits or as victims of an irresponsible uncle who handed them over to the care of an emotionally unstable young woman, they are touching in their helplessness. The governess sees them at first as perfect vessels of purity and beauty, thus establishing their effectiveness as foils for her vision of the ghosts as the embodiment of corruption and ugliness. James is careful never to permit the reader to forget that beneath the surface of the governess' unrealistic appraisal

14. Two recent additions to the classic controversy are *An Anatomy of "The Turn of the Screw"* by Thomas Mabry Cranfil and Robert Lanier Clark Jr. (Austin, 1965) and The Norton Critical Edition, *The Turn of the Screw: An Authoritative Text, Backgrounds and Sources, Essays in Criticism,* ed. Robert Kimbrough (New York, 1966). Aside from suggesting that the governess is suffering from "hypnogenesis," Cranfil and Clark do not offer any striking new interpretation of the tale. Their documentation of the controversy, however, is comprehensive. The Norton Edition contains James's final authoritative text. It offers textual history; background and sources; early, major, and recent criticism (among these, two heretofore unpublished essays). The Norton Edition, in conjunction with Willen's *Casebook,* is invaluable to the student of "The Turn of the Screw."

of Flora and Miles (*no* children could be as perfect as the governess declares them to be) there exist credible little characters. If the young woman's interpretation of their behavior can be called into question, the behavior itself never can. At no point in the story does James have Flora or Miles *do* anything that might not be construed as perfectly normal behavior for children of their class and obvious intelligence. The reader can never, with any degree of certainty, say what the children really are, only what they could possibly be. Miles could be the soul of corruption, and, by the same token, he could be a typical little Victorian gentleman who minds his manners, is precocious enough to call his governess "my dear," and naughty enough to be expelled from school. Flora could be the essence of depravity, but she could, just as well, be an absorbed child playing with her boat, an anxious little girl leaving her bed in search of her governess, or a badly frightened infant responding to incomprehensible and threatening behavior on the part of the adult who cares for her. None of the acts committed by the children and endowed by the governess with overtones of deception, corruption, or wickedness are, in and of themselves, necessarily so motivated. Whether Flora and Miles are evil or not, whether they actually see the ghosts and have formed an unholy alliance with them or not, depends entirely on the habit of mind and emotional make-up of the individual reader. And it is precisely this freedom of interpretation—this scope for the unfettered play of the imaginative faculty—that James was seeking for his reader. He succeeded because Miles and Flora are credible as Victorian upper-class children; their credibility filters through the distorting screen of the governess' perception of them. Because we sense their normality, we can accept the idea that their behavior could have a deeper and more ominous significance.

Young children in James's fiction have progressed from "unseeing" to "seeing," from "unknowing" to "knowing," and from passivity to active engagement, until, in this final tale in which young children figure, there is no clearly defined limit to what they could conceivably "see," "know," or "do." In a larger philosophical sense—and in James's fiction there is always the broader implication to be considered—the novelist's treatment of the children and of the governess in "The Turn of the Screw" serves as a comment on the essential ambiguity of the human condition and the interchangeability of appearance and reality in a world where most questions do not have final and irrevocable answers. A recognition of this aspect of James's thought is not to suggest that he took a relativistic attitude toward human behavior or that he withheld value judgments. His fictional and nonfictional pronouncements testify to the fact that quite the contrary was true. But it was with a full understanding of the impossibility of the task that he consistently sought the reconciliation of opposites within a clearly defined moral framework. In "The Turn of the Screw" James has given dramatic form to this dilemma of human experience. He tells us in his preface that the tale was meant as "an exercise of the imagination unassisted, unassociated—playing the game, making the score, in the phrase of our sporting day, off its own bat." As it turned out, James's little "exercise" occasioned a response in his reader which suggests a more substantial function for his ghostly fable. In setting out to explore the ambiguous nature of good and evil and the process by which true knowledge is acquired, the novelist touched upon a fundamental truth of human existence. Virtue and vice coexist in each of us. The quality of the individual perception is what truly counts, for both good and evil reside in the eye of the beholder. Appropriately the author chose two children and an adolescent to dramatize his theme of the co-presence of virtue and vice in one entity, because it is a truth of human nature which must be assimilated before the claim to maturity can be made.

With the young telegraphist of *In the Cage* (1898), (*Complete Tales*, X) James makes the reader privy to the inner life of a curious and sensitive girl who is on the brink of maturity. Unlike the governess, the little telegraphist perceives reality; her problem is to make peace with it. The charm of this sensitive and oddly neglected tales lies in James's delicate rendering of the girl's response to a world by which she is beguiled but which she can never hope to be a part of. Hers is indeed a fine consciousness (perhaps, at times, too fine for credibility) and the reader is exposed to every nuance of it as the girl stands apart, as it were, and takes note of her own need to escape from the reality of a humdrum existence. James's heroine lives vicariously through the messages she is called upon to send in her capacity as telegraphist in a corner of Cocker's grocery store in the heart of Mayfair. The fashionable people who frequent the establishment afford her a glimpse, through their telegraphed messages, into the *grand monde* and form the basis for the girl's self-created illusion. We meet her at that juncture in her life when she must choose between her fiance, Mr. Mudge, a thrifty and ambitious grocery cleark who will someday have a shop of his own, and a life of unrealistic daydreams about a world she can never with any dignity enter. The alternatives are there at the outset; the dramatic action consists of the young girl's gradual acceptance of herself and her life situation. The maturing process is hastened through her involvement, via the telegrams she sends for the people concerned, in an adulterous affair between Captain Everard and Lady Bradeen. Because she was so interested in their lives, the little telegraphist is able to recall the text of a crucial telegram thus saving Everard and his aristocratic mistress from the disgrace of an open scandal. The incident catapults the adolescent into maturity. It teaches her that the aristocratic world has its fair share of corruption and vice, and she sees it for what it is; she meets her hero face to face and realizes that he has feet of clay. Most important of all, she is given the opportunity to make a moral choice when she becomes aware that a relationship with Captain Everard other than that of telegraphist and client is a very real possibility for her. There is a parallel action in the story of Mrs. Jordan, the shabby genteel widow and confidant of the girl who, like the young telegraphist, seeks to escape her mundane existence by arranging flowers for the aristocracy and who dreams of making a brilliant marriage via the servants' entrance. The older and younger woman both realize the futility of their unrealistic aspirations and make peace with things as they are.

In the Cage is a subtle, gentle tale of growth through perception, of the successful synthesis of emotion and intellect, of the achievement of identity through self-knowledge. The youthful telegraphist captures the imagination of the reader at the outset; she is so keenly aware of her own needs:

It had occurred to her early that in her position—that of a young person spending, in framed and wired confinement, the life of a guinea-pig or a magpie—she should know a great many persons without their recognising the acquaintance. That made it an emotion the more lively—though singularly rare and always, even then, with opportunity still very much smothered—to see any one come in whom she knew, as she called it, outside, and who could add something to the poor identity of her function. (*Complete Tales*, X, 139)

We never worry about the sensitive young girl in the cage; we know that somehow she will come through all right. The question becomes rather what she will make of "the queer extension of her experience, the double life that, in the cage, she grew at last to lead." Because she is so intensely alive, so unusually perceptive, she makes the most of her experience; she transforms it into the stuff of maturity. Like the ideal creative artist James envisioned, the young girl in the cage is "one of the people on whom nothing is lost." Indeed there are several striking parallels between the novelist's conception of the gifted writer and his adolescent telegraphist. Echoes of James's pronouncements on the function of the creative imagination can be noted throughout the story: "She had surrendered herself moreover, of late, to a certain expansion of her consciousness . . . there were more impressions to be gathered and really—for it came to that—more life to be led." (*Complete Tales*, X, 143)

In his essay on the art of fiction, James suggests that the truly creative writer will have the "power to guess the unseen from the seen, to trace the implications of things to judge the whole piece by the pattern . . . this cluster of gifts may almost be said to constitute experience and they occur in country and in town and in the most differing stages of education." The little telegraphist has such attributes in abundance. "When she noticed, she noticed; that was what it came to." In his biography James speaks of his own youthful feeling: "Just to *be* somewhere—almost anywhere would do—and somehow receive an impression or an accession, feel a relation or a vibration." [15]

Of the girl in the cage he tells us: "The great thing was the flashes, the quick revivals, absolute accidents all, and neither to be counted on nor to be resisted. Some one had only sometimes to put in a penny for a stamp, and the whole thing was upon her. She was so absurdly constructed that these were literally the moments that made up—made up for the long stiffness of sitting there in the stocks. . . ." (*Complete Tales*, X, 143) The telegraph cage becomes a fount of imagination for the impressionable young girl—"But who," said James in his autobiography, "shall count the sources at which an intense young fancy (when a young fancy *is* intense) capriciously, absurdly drinks?" [16]

Maturation is closely associated in James's mind with the development of the artist. He demanded the same course and the same standards for the evolving adult as he did for the maturing writer. In his presentation of the growth of the caged young woman, James has, in a very real sense, created a metaphor for the growth of the artist. As the novelist converted his impressions into the art of fiction, so the little telegraphist transforms hers into an acceptance of the conditions of life: "Where was one's pride and one's passion when the real way to judge of one's luck was by making not the wrong, but the right, comparison? Before she had again gathered herself to go she felt very small and cautious and thankful." (*Complete Tales*, X, 237) When the young girl faces the reality of her situation in Mrs. Jordan's little parlor, she has finally con-

15. Henry James, *A Small Boy and Others* (New York, 1913), p. 25.
   16. Ibid., p. 347.

verted her experience and her impressions into a philosophy of life that will make it viable for her.

If the cage shelters the girl's creative imagination, it
is, at the same time, emblematic of a special kind of un-
reality, one in which the passive observer of men and
manners can find refuge from threatening experiences.
The telegraphist has her moment of confrontation with
a very real aspect of life when she understands the nature of Captain Everard's interest in her. The prospect
of an intimate relationship with her idol terrifies her:
". . . to be in the cage had suddenly become her safety,
and she was literally afraid of the alternate self who
might be waiting outside. *He* might be waiting; it was he
who was her alternate self, and of him she was afraid.
The most extraordinary change had taken place in her
from the moment of her catching the impression he
seemed to have returned on purpose to give her." (*Complete Tales*, X, 213–14)

To be the passive spectator, set off by the cage from
active involvement with life, had its advantages. The reality of a sexual-relationship with Captain Everard was
more frightening to her than the reality of life with Mr.
Mudge. The biographical parallel is too obvious to need
elaboration: "The evidence of Henry James's life points
to a curiously paradoxical element in his personality: he
was an active and masculine individual who finding direct
action impossible—and with this direct expression of his
individuality—realized this activity and individuality
through a prodigiously creative and highly productive
art, while remaining to all appearances passive in the
extreme." [17]

Like his young heroine, James found freedom from
anxiety in the cage of his creative imagination. But for
the adolescent telegraphist more than fear is involved;
there is the necessity to make a sensible, realistic, rea-
soned and, in James's terms, therefore a moral choice.
The perceptive young girl meets the problem squarely

17. Leon Edel, *Henry James*, Vol. I, *The Untried Years: 1843–1870*
(New York, 1953), p. 65.

and with a maximum of self-awareness: "This change was the tribute of her fear—the result of a change in himself as to which she needed no more explanation than his mere face vividly gave her; strange though it was to find an element of deterrence in the object that she regarded as the most beautiful in the world. He had taken it from her in the Park that night that she wanted him not to propose to her to sup; but he had put away the lesson by this time—he practically proposed supper every time he looked at her." (*Complete Tales*, X, 214)

There are levels of reality, and for the lucid young girl, about to enter adulthood and assume the responsibility it implied, the reality of Mr. Mudge and their "own little house" was the only possible one. After her moment of triumph in the cage of Cocker's, she takes the only appropriate step out into the real world. There remains for her to take the measure of her own flight from reality against that of Mrs. Jordan's. The "brown fog" of self-delusion that permeates that lady's little parlor is dispelled for both women when Mrs. Jordan confesses that she is to marry Mr. Drake, who is, after all, nothing more than a butler—"what our heroine saw and felt for in the whole business was the vivid reflection of her own dreams and delusions and her own return to reality." (*Complete Tales*, X, 236)

The adolescent telegraphist's story is told in muted tones. She is not called upon to make courageous renunciations or take an heroic stand. But what she lacks in grandeur she compensates for in delicacy of feeling and acuteness of perception. Perhaps more than any of James's younger heroines, she illuminates certain aspects of her creator's personality and gives voice to some of his most basic assumptions about the process of growing up. Her avid curiosity is tempered by self-consciousness, restraint, and moral integrity. If there is less ambiguity, and consequently less excitement, surrounding her, she sheds a gentle light of her own on James's convictions about what constitutes true maturity in the emerging adult.

The governess and the telegraphist are antithetical in

that they represent the obverse and converse of the proposition that true knowledge derives from maximum consciousness and a vision of reality free from distortion. This is a theme James was to bring to its most complete and triumphant realization in the portrait of his most complex adolescent, Nanda Brookenham, the logical successor to the deluded young governess and the unheroic little telegraphist.

CHAPTER IX

Nanda

James's interest in the intellectual and spiritual development of the young, which began with Nora Lambert of *Watch and Ward* in 1871, is given its ultimate expression in his fictional representation of the troubled adolescent, Nanda Brookenham of *The Awkward Age* (1899).[1] In this novel he offers his most complex and comprehensive epistemological statement. He defines the "well-brought-up" young girl, circumscribes familial responsibility and characterizes the society in which maximum growth is possible. He creates, finally, his own species of *jeune fille* and contrasts her directly with her more traditional sister. All James's themes of childhood and adolescence and all his fictional young people converge in his rendering of Nanda. She is the novelist's final and vigorous affirmation of the moral superiority of the exposed innocent. Where Nora was shallow, Nanda is profound; where Pansy wanted courage, Nanda possesses it in abundance; where the governess lacked insight and discrimination, Nanda's vision of reality is penetrating in the extreme; where the girl in the cage lacked stature, Nanda emerges as spiritually and intellectually larger than life. Nanda Brookenham is James's tribute to adolescence as Maisie Farange was his panegyric to childhood. The curious, wondering little girl gives way to the alert young woman who, because of her fine consciousness, is able to face the evil of her world with equanimity and make the choice that will ensure her moral superiority.

1. Henry James, *The Awkward Age* (New York, 1904). This edition, rather than the New York Edition, is used for references in this chapter.

There are striking parallels in characterization and motif between *Watch and Ward* and James's last work on this theme; and differences in emphasis and treatment chart the evolution of the novelist's sensibility during the twenty-eight years separating the two works. The naïve eroticism of the early novel has become internalized in the later one; it is indicated rather than overtly (if unconsciously) stated. The incestuous overtones of the father-daughter relationship, in the novel of 1871, is apparent only by inference in the later work; it is sensed beneath the surface of the manners and mores. The moral and emotional climate of the adolescent—given slight treatment in *Watch and Ward*—plays a dominant role in *The Awkward Age*. More than the similarity of first initials and analagous relationships with the men in their lives relate Nora and Nanda. Both young women express a sexual fantasy of rejection deeply rooted in the personality of their creator, but a change in the nature of the love object has taken place. The ordinary young girl of the first tale, with her immature notions of a hero on a white horse, has been transformed into the realistic young woman of the later work. Between 1871 and 1899, James had achieved an emotional and intellectual ripeness that enabled him to convert a youthful day dream into mature art.

James first mentions the idea for *The Awkward Age* in a notebook entry of March 4, 1895. Although the notation is a short one, all the elements necessary for James's final statement on the education of the young girl are incorporated in it. "The idea of the little London girl," he writes, "who grows up to 'sit with' the free-talking modern young mother—reaches 17, 18, etc.—comes out—and, not marrying, has to 'be there'. . . ."[2] Thus the scene is set for the young girl's exposure; he is not yet certain, however, what form it will take. ". . . and, though the conversation is supposed to be expurgated for her, [she] inevitably hears, overhears, guesses, follows, takes in, becomes acquainted with, horror." In the novel no one

2. *The Notebooks of Henry James*, ed. F. O. Matthiessen and Kenneth B. Murdock (New York, 1962), p. 192.

takes the trouble to "expurgate" the conversation for Nanda's sake, and the "horror" is right there for her to see in the behavior of her reprehensible family. In this first entry James envisions the direct contrast that he was to dramatize between the two educational systems that had so long engaged his imagination. "There may be the contrasted clever, *avisée* foreign or foreignized friend or sister, who has married her daughter, very virtuously and very badly, unhappily, just to get her out of the atmosphere of her own talk and entourage—and takes *my* little lady to task for her inferior system and inferior virtue." The foreignized friend became the hypocritical Duchess whose concern for her niece, Aggie, is rooted in her own snobbery. In the novel Nanda's mother and Aggie's aunt are both guilty of parental dereliction, and the girls, emblematic of the two approaches to education, are placed in opposition. Aggie represents the sheltered innocent, Nanda "the little girl who is conscious and aware. 'I am modern—I'm supposed to know—I'm not a *jeune fille*'. . . ." Between the notebook entry and the finished work James has shifted his emphasis to the question of parental culpability.

His notation continues: "Something in this really, I think—especially if one makes it to take in something of the question of the non-marrying of girls, the desperation of mothers, the whole alteration of manners . . . and tone, while our theory of the participation, the *presence* of the young, remains unaffected by it." His brief discussion of what he planned to project in his tale is comprehensive. He seemed, from the first, to know exactly what direction he would take. I believe this to be so because James had, since his first observation of the *jeune fille* and her mother in 1876, returned again and again to the question in his fictional as well as nonfictional writing; he had had ample time to arrive at a formulation of his ideas on the subject. On December 21, 1895, in his second and final notebook reference to the novel, he wrote, *"The Awkward Age:* to be completely ciphered out. It exists as yet only in a brief former note and in my head—but I can produce it the moment I sit down to it—certainly with the help of my former note."[3] He could produce it so easily because it had been taking form for twenty-three years. It was merely a question now of finding the appropriate form. As had been the case with *What Maisie Knew*, James was concerned that his "real little subject" should have the proper setting. As in the earlier novel he became fascinated with the technical problems involved—an indication of the salience, for him, of the theme. Predictably, the "short tale" developed into a lengthy novel. It was serialized in *Harper's Weekly*, October 1, 1898, through January 7, 1899, and was published in book form April 25, 1899. James blamed the failure of the novel on his complicated "scenic" method. Actually the novel is an admirable example of form illuminating theme. The self-revelation of character possible by the use of the scenic (or dramatic) form—the novel is almost all dialogue—establishes effectively and concretely the worlds between which Nanda must ultimately choose.

In *The Awkward Age* the novelist has limited his field of observation to that period in a young girl's life in which childhood must be left behind but adulthood has not yet been achieved. "*The Awkward Age*," he tells us in his preface, "is precisely a study of one of those curtailed or extended periods of tension and apprehension. . . ."[4] It is quite clear *what* Nanda "sees," just as her interpretation of what she observes is unfailingly accurate. Here the novelist is examining more exclusively and in greater depth the process by which knowledge is acquired, and he is attempting to find the governing laws that determine inner growth. Nora Lambert gave the first indication of James's interest in the educative process, and with Pansy Osmond we noted the beginnings of a specific philosophy of education. With Nanda we begin to see that the adolescent mind is significantly affected by the quality of the minds to which it is exposed. It is a self-evident truth that the young spirit draws sustenance from the society that nurtures it. While emotional and

3. Ibid., p. 233.
4. Henry James, *The Art of the Novel*, ed. R. P. Blackmur (New York, 1934), p. 103.

spiritual wholeness lie in the fullest possible perception
of life, the quality of the mind exposed to these perceptions will, after all, determine the value of the insight.
"The truth is," said James in his preface to the novel,
"that what a happy thought has to give depends immensely on the general turn of the mind capable of it, and
on the fact that its loyal entertainer . . . is terribly at the
mercy of his mind." [5] Superior "vessels of consciousness"
are, after all, few and far between, and the Morgans,
Maisies, and Nandas of this world are called upon to pay
a heavy price.

In *The Awkward Age* James deliberately and carefully
scrutinizes and anatomizes a segment of society which is
remiss in fulfilling its obligations to the young. The problems connected with Nanda's growth illuminate and comment upon a society so corrupt that it can no longer distinguish between good and evil. Through the young girl's
insight, the reader is given a probing account of the decadence and depravity that lie behind the "good talk" in her
mother's drawing room.

Nanda lives in a morally dislocated world in which
virtue and vice are so thoroughly confused that only a
superior mind can penetrate the falsities and hypocrisies
which permeate the very air she breathes. Like Morgan
Moreen, Nanda "sees" her family's moral turpitude and
is ashamed; unlike the doomed young boy, she is able to
successfully assimilate the knowledge, repudiate the society that her parents represent, and find a better moral
climate in which to make a life for herself.

The Brookenhams are the Moreens of "The Pupil" but
enlarged and expanded to fit the larger frame of a full-
length novel. They emerge as a subtle, even sinister, combination of young Morgan's family and the Faranges of
Maisie. The Brookenhams have the intellectual pretensions and social credentials to assure free entry into the
drawing rooms and country houses of the English aristocracy which the Moreens coveted and lacked, but the
value system of both families is fundamentally indis-

5. Ibid., p. 101.

tinguishable. The "chatter" that dominates the world of the Faranges becomes the "good talk" in the Brookenham set; both are characterized by malicious gossip and frivolous character assassination. Mrs. Brookenham is oddly reminiscent, as well, of Gilbert Osmond of *The Portrait of a Lady*. Like Osmond's "taste," Mrs. Brook's "wit" becomes a dominant value, an end in itself, and, as was the case with Pansy's father, the positive attribute hides the most ruthless and destructive kind of egotism.

The mothers of James's three stories of childhood and adolescence—"The Pupil," *What Maisie Knew*, and *The Awkward Age*—are all basically derelict in their duty toward their children, but the novelist's characterization of them gains complexity and subtlety as James moves from the short story to the broader canvas of the novel. While Mrs. Moreen is merely shabby, pathetic, and thoughtless in her futile effort to become a part of the aristocratic world, Mrs. Brook is awesome in her capacity for manipulation, ruthless in her effort to protect her position as wit and sage of her circle, and relentless in her determination to keep for herself the young man her daughter loves. Like Ida Farange, Mrs. Brook assumes terrifying proportions, but she is more subtly rendered than Maisie's mother; she is more devious than Ida; her transgressions lurk behind a beguiling façade of beauty, wit, and charm: "She had about her the pure light of youth—would always have it; her head, her figure, her flexibility, her flickering color, her lovely silly eyes, her natural quavering tone all played together toward this effect by some trick that had never yet been exposed." (*Awkward Age*, p. 36)

Mrs. Brook's youthful appearance belies her tired inner cynicism; her "silly eyes" misrepresent the calculating mind behind them. She is universally admired in her circle for her unusual insight, her ability to appraise a situation accurately. But her "notorious perception" represents a perversion of the cognitive faculty. Through Mrs. Brookenham, James is saying that perception without a moral frame of reference to which it may be related is not only useless but destructive. In this sense Mrs.

Brook is the antithesis of her daughter and serves as foil to her. Nanda is emblematic of true vision, her mother of false.

The fathers of *Portrait*, "The Pupil," *Maisie*, and *The Awkward Age* are ineffectual as are so many Jamesian men, but the novelist found the trait most reprehensible in the male parent. Edward Brookenham's blandness is the measure of his lack of involvement with humanity, his selfishness, and ultimately his immorality. Just as Mr. Moreen's "worldliness" covers his irresponsibility and his self-delusion, so Brookenham's evasiveness hides his placid indifference and essential egotism. James's physical description of Edward Brookenham is remarkable for its incisive delineation of an uninvolved, ineffectual husband and father:

He had a pale, cold face, marked and made regular, made even in a manner handsome, by a hardness of line in which, oddly, there was no significance, no accent. Clean shaven, slightly bald, with unlighted gray eyes and a mouth that gave the impression of not working easily, he suggested a stippled drawing by an inferior master. . . . If anything particular had finally been expected from him it might have been a summary or an explanation of the things he had always not said. . . . (*Awkward Age*, p. 55)

When Brookenham suspects that his wastrel son is borrowing money from their friends which he does not intend to repay, he decides that he will not inquire about it; "it will be such a beastly bore if he admits it." The air of cynicism and pseudo-sophistication which hangs over the discussion with his wife, the accord both reach on how best to use their friends in order to maintain a standard of living they cannot afford, is as immoral as Ida and Beale Farange's passionate resolve to use Maisie to carry on their feud. The Faranges are undisciplined and irrational, the Brookenhams coldly calculating and cynically devoid of feeling. Their deliberate inhumanity is frightening. People capable of feeling hate, like the Faranges, might after all be equally capable of feeling love; people devoid of any feeling, like the Brookenhams, are scarcely human and beyond redemption.

Harold Brookenham is Morgan Moreen's brother,

Ulick, fully rendered. Like Randolph C. Miller, Daisy's "spoiled" little brother, he has never benefited from parental guidance and discipline; he has inevitably grown into an irresponsible and less "charming" extension of his parents. Unlike Randolph, however, he inspires no feeling of pity. He is thoroughly reprehensible: "He was small and had a slight stoop, which somehow gave him character—a character somewhat of the insidious sort, carried out in the acuteness, difficult to trace to a source, of his smooth fair face, whose lines were all curves and its expression all needles. He had the voice of a man of forty, and was dressed . . . with an air of experience that seemed to match it." (*Awkward Age*, p. 35)

Harold Brookenham does indeed borrow money he cannot repay, spends weekends in homes where he is not wanted, and finally becomes the social "rage" by pandering to women who are bored with their husbands. He emerges as more despicable than the people who helped form him because he has fully realized all their vagaries. Harold stands in direct contrast to his sister. He is the logical product of his mother's set. The course he follows is inevitale because he does not have the saving grace of awareness, empathy, and intelligence. He is the spectre of what Nanda could have become had she not been endowed with her extraordinary sympathy and understanding of human fallibility.

The central problem in the novel is the question of Nanda's "exposure"—as a young, innocent, and unmarried girl—to the intrigue, malicious gossip, and hostile witticisms that characterize the atmosphere of her mother's "impossible" drawing room. As was often the case with James, his original aim was the modest exploration of the tensions felt by a young girl and those around her when she finds herself in the no man's land between schoolroom and drawing room: ". . . the 'sitting downstairs,' from a given date, of the merciless maiden previously perched aloft could easily be felt as a crisis. This crisis, and the sense for it in those whom it most concerns, has to confess itself courageously the prime propulsive force of 'The Awkward Age.' Such a matter might well make a scant show for a 'thick book,' and no thick book, but just a quite charmingly thin one, was in fact originally dreamt of." [6]

As it turned out, however, in the problem of Nanda's "sitting downstairs," James created a metaphor for the larger issue of a society judged and found wanting. Through the young girl's luminous vision, the author calls into question a world that confuses propriety with morality, compromises integrity for personal gain, and places greater value on meaningless convention than on human affection. Nanda's "exposure" is the occasion, as well, for the juxtaposition of the values inherent in an old, traditional, and stable society against those of a new, modern, and changing one. The world in which Nanda grows up has lost its moral footing in the process of adapting to rapid and bewildering social change. The conventions of an earlier age have survived, but the integrity that gives substance to them has disappeared, leaving the empty shell of manners and mores and an ethical code that is observed more in the breach than in the practice. Form without substance leads inevitably to hypocrisy and eventually to loss of self-esteem. In the private adherence to principle and in the personal ability to perceive the true, the real, and the lasting values in life (James argues through character and situation in *The Awkward Age*) lies the hope for a morally reconstructed society that will give meaning to the lives of its individual members. The doubt that a jaded social group casts upon Nanda's innocence dramatizes the Jamesian preoccupation with the difficulty of distinguishing between appearance and reality. The seeming failure of Nanda emerges as success and the seeming success of Aggie is revealed as failure. This notion of the essential paradox that lies at the heart of man's perception of reality is concretized in the characterization of the gossips so concerned with Nanda's "exposure."

The habitués of Mrs. Brookenham's drawing room at Buckingham Crescent, each in his own way, incarnate

6. Ibid., p. 100.

some form of moral obfuscation; each contributes to the general feeling of decadence and exemplifies a specific dereliction that contributes to the disintegration of a clearly defined ethical code of behavior. The Duchess' "colorless hair" and "passionless forehead" become the correlative for her moral neutrality. She is quite untroubled by her own illicit involvement with Lord Petherton while at the same time terribly preoccupied with preserving her niece Aggie's innocence and deploring Nanda's exposure to the realities of life. Lord Petherton —with his "unpleasant brutality" and his "handsome parade of carnivorous teeth"—epitomizes the duplicity of the Brookenham set. Not only does he freely sponge on his rich friend, Mitchy, but he has no compunction about compromising his wife, having already been her mother's lover. Vanderbank, with whom Nanda is inexplicably in love, is so afraid of his own moral deficiencies, one of which is his questionable attachment to Mrs. Brook, that he uses the empty convention of the double standard to avoid Nanda's penetrating assessment of his character. He rejects Nanda ostensibly because she "knows" too much to be a socially acceptable wife; actually this is his rationale for his inability to face himself.

Two characters in the novel understand and appreciate Nanda. Mr. Longdon, the older counterpart of Roger Lawrence in *Watch and Ward*, was in love with Nanda's grandmother. He comes to realize, through his contact with the girl, that integrity can coexist with a knowledge of evil in one individual. Mitchy, who is in love with Nanda, has known it all along. Neither of these admirers, however, can help Nanda achieve a fulfilled life. Mr. Longdon, representative of the old order, must, of necessity, turn his back on the world of Buckingham Crescent; Mitchy, representative of the new, remains impotently a part of it and watches resignedly, hopelessly (albeit perceptively) from the side lines as the falsities and hypocrisies are perpetuated through his wife, Aggie, and Nanda's brother, Harold. Like so many Jamesian heroes, Mitchy lacks the strength to take effective action and withdraws from the arena. Nanda must work out her own salvation. Thus the novelist underscores his thesis that hope for society lies ultimately in the cultivation of the individual consciousness and the supreme attribute is the ability to see things through.

In order to dramatize his theme more effectively and economically, James has created a group of antithetical characters; their function is to illuminate different aspects of the paradox of good in evil and evil in good. The most significant polarity is set up between the two adolescent girls. Nanda is seemingly lacking in virtue because of her too early exposure to the sophistication of Mrs. Brook's set. Aggie is apparently virtuous because she is the product of a sheltered education. Yet Nanda emerges as truly pure while Aggie all too quickly loses an ephemeral innocence grounded in an unrealistic view of life. Vanderbank is a young sophisticate who appears to know and accept the realities of life, and Mr. Longdon is a conservative of the old school who seems to reject any notion of sophistication. Yet, in the final analysis, Vanderbank is shown as a captive of his own rigidity, and Mr. Longdon comes, under Nanda's tutelage, to exhibit a flexibility of which the younger man is incapable. Nanda is emblematic of the "new," thinking young adolescent who has gained perspective through an expanded consciousness and the ability to realistically appraise the world around her. She tries to explain herself to Van:

"Girls understand now. It has got to be faced. . . . Even Mr. Longdon admits that."
Vanderbank wondered, "You mean you talk over with him—"
"The subject of girls? Why we scarcely discuss anything else. . . ." "But you mean," Vanderbank asked, "that he recognizes the inevitable change—?"
"He can't shut his eyes to the facts. He sees we're quite a different thing." (*Awkward Age*, pp. 286–87)

Vanderbank, however, is unable to free himself from old prejudices and hollow snobbery. Mr. Longdon, the traditionalist, is capable of making the distinction between false propriety and true virtue while Van, the would-be modernist, is not.

James's adolescent, Nanda, is more fully realized than was his younger heroine, Maisie, because the portrait of the older girl has greater psychological verisimilitude. The role of parental egotism and indifference in the formation of Nanda's character is given more subtle treatment than in the earlier novel. The relationship between mother and daughter is suggested rather than stated. "The two were confronted as closely as persons may be when it is only one of them who looks at the other." (*Awkward Age,* pp. 262–63) Mrs. Brookenham's lack of feeling for her daughter, her fundamental indifference to the girl's needs is sufficiently but indirectly exposed:

That they *were* as good friends as if Nanda had not been her daughter was a truth that no passage between them might fail in one way or another to illustrate. Nanda had gathered up, for that matter, early in life, a flower of maternal wisdom: "People talk about the conscience, but it seems to me one must just bring it up to a certain point and leave it there. You can let your conscience alone if you're nice to the second house-maid." Mrs. Brook was as "nice" to Nanda as she was to Sarah Curd—which involved, as may easily be imagined, the happiest condition for Sarah. (*Awkward Age,* p. 264)

What such treatment involved for Nanda is precisely the hub of James's tale. It is the basis for the young girl's highly developed perceptive faculty, which, as is usually the case with the novelist's abused young people, evolved through her need to protect herself in the face of indifference and neglect. Her mother's behavior determines her response to Mr. Longdon. He, perhaps, will offer the emotional security she never had:

"*Does* he, my dear, want to marry you?"
  "Yes—to all sorts of ridiculous people."
  "But I mean, would you take *him*?"
  Nanda, rising, met the question with a short ironic "Yes!" that showed her first impatience. "It's so charming being liked," she went on, "without being approved." (*Awkward Age,* p. 270)

Mr. Longdon's approval becomes a necessity for Nanda, but it must be forthcoming on her own terms. For the first time in her young life, she is determined to be completely and unequivocally accepted for what she is. This need motivates her to undertake the "education" of Mr. Longdon:

> ". . . what it comes to seems to be that I'm really what you may call adopting *him*—gradually showing him that, as I couldn't possibly have been different, and as also, of course, one can't keep giving up, the only way is for him not to mind and to take me just as I am." (*Awkward Age*, pp. 270–71)

The ironic reversal of roles in the educative process that held such peculiar fascination for James appears again and again in his rendering of child-adult relations. The first unmistakable projection of it is to be found in *Watch and Ward.* Just as Mr. Longdon feels inadequate in the face of Nanda's "acuteness" and "profundity," so "Roger was forever suspecting [Nora] of a deeper penetration than his own and hanging his head with an odd mixture of pride and humility. Her quick perception at times made him feel irretrievably dull and antiquated." (*Watch and Ward*, pp. 67–68) Nora Lambert began the education of her elders in 1871; Morgan and Maisie partially achieved it in the early 1890's; and Nanda Brookenham completed it at the end of the decade by bringing the older man completely around to her view of life, but the price she is prepared to pay for her success is celibacy. If she cannot "educate" a husband for herself, she will settle for a father.

Like Morgan Moreen of "The Pupil," Nanda is painfully aware of her family's irresponsibility. "Well then, with everyone helping us, all round, aren't we a lovely family? We seem to be all living more or less on other people, all immensely 'beholden'." (*Awkward Age*, p. 290) Unlike Morgan, however, she is not destroyed by her insight. Van may not perceive it, but she, at least, knows that Harold is more truly their mother's child than she will ever be.

Character illuminates theme in James's handling of the complicated relationship between Nanda and Van. The young man does not distinguish between manners and morality, form and content, shadow and substance. Because Nanda can make that distinction he is oddly re-

pelled by her, and the young woman takes the full measure of his aversion:

> "I remember you once telling me that I must take in things
> at my pores. . . ."
>   "And when did I make this extraordinary charge?"
>   "Ah then," said Nanda, "you admit it *is* a charge.
>   It was a long time ago—when I was a little girl. Which
> made it worse!" she dropped. . . . "Ah, not worse—better!"
> She thought a moment. "Because in that case I mightn't have
> understood? But that I do understand is just what you've
> always meant." " 'Always,' my dear Nanda? I feel somehow,"
> he rejoined very kindly, "as if you overwhelmed me!" "You
> 'feel' as if I did—but the reality is just that I don't. The day
> I overwhelm you, Mr. Van—!" (*Awkward Age*, pp. 285–86)

Nanda's perspicacity is exhibited all the more clearly
when it is shown in contrast to Van's lack of imagination.
Her accurate assessment of Van's character and the
source of his antipathy toward her reflects rare wisdom
in one so young. His failure to appreciate her humanity,
his embarrassment in the presence of truth defines him
for us:

> "It's the tone and the current and the effect of all the others
> that push you along. . . . If such things are contagious, as
> every one says, you prove it perhaps as much as anyone. But
> you don't begin"—she continued, blandly enough, to work it
> out for him; "or you can't, at least, originally have begun.
> Anyone would know that now—from the teriffic effect I see
> I produce on you by talking this way. There it is—it's all out
> before one knows it, isn't it, and I can't help it any more than
> you can, can I?" So she appeared to put it to him, with some-
> thing in her lucidity that would have been infinitely touching;
> a strange, grave, calm consciousness of their common doom
> and of what in especial in it would be worst for herself.
> (*Awkward Age*, p. 288)

There is irony and pathos in the girl's grasp of the fact
that Van, not she, has been contaminated by contact with
Mrs. Brook's set. Van's final interview with Nanda in her
"redecorated and rededicated room upstairs" is rendered
with great sensitivity. The two characters are finally and
clearly juxtaposed—Vanderbank, the weak, irresponsible, hypocritical anti-hero; Nanda, intelligent, humane,
mature. Tension mounts during the course of the scene as
Nanda valiantly attempts to reach Van's heart and mind

and as he persists in his determined effort to block all avenues of communication between them: "Practically, however, he would let her tell him nothing; his almost aggressive friendly optimism clung so to references of short range. "Don't mention it, please. It's too charming of you to squeeze me in. To see *you*, moreover, does me good. Quite distinct good. And your writing me touched me—oh, but really. There were all sorts of old things in it." Then he broke out, once more, on her books, one of which for some minutes past, he had held in his hand." (*Awkward Age*, p. 419)

The scene builds to its climax as Van's discomfort becomes more acute and his tone of friendly banter more strident. The ultimate irony is achieved when Nanda, like Maisie before her, realizes that she must shoulder the responsibility for Van's rejection of her; like her younger predecessor, she must assume the role of disclaimer. And because Nanda is more responsible, more compassionate, and stronger than Van, she effects the complete reversal of roles for which his behavior silently pleads: "To force upon him an awkwardness was like forcing a disfigurement or a hurt, so that at the end of a minute during which the expression of her face became a kind of uplifted view of her opportunity, she arrived at the appearance of having changed places with him and of their being together precisely in order that he—not she—should be let down easily. (*Awkward Age*, p. 421)

But Nanda's self-imposed obligation does not end here. Not only must she let Van down easily, she must ensure his continued devotion to her mother. "You *can't* know how much you are to her. You're more to her, I verily believe, than anyone *ever* was . . . you mustn't too much leave her alone. *Don't!*" (*Awkward Age*, pp. 426, 429) Instead of Mrs. Brook (in the manner of the *mère de famille*) providing a husband for Nanda, in the perverted world of Buckingham Crescent, the daughter provides a lover (albeit a platonic one) for her mother. And for the final irony, James has Van ask Nanda to "square" him with Mr. Longdon. Not having had the courage to face the old gentleman and tell him honestly his reasons for not accepting Nanda and the dowry Longdon was offering, he leaves it to the girl to show the old man "somehow or other that I'm *not* a brute." (*Awkward Age*, p. 430)

Nanda's unusual perception, her ability to evaluate herself as well as others, ensures her defeat with the man she loves for reasons that become apparent as the characterization of Vanderbank develops. Less clear is the question of Nanda's relationship with Mitchy, one of James's more complicated anti-heroes:

> It was written all over him that he had judged, once for all, his personal case, and that as his character . . . deprived him of the resource of shyness and shade, the effect of comedy might not escape him if secured by a real plunge. There was comedy therefore in the form of his pot-hat and the color of his spotted shirt, in the systematic disagreement, above all, of his coat, waistcoat and trousers. It was only on long acquaintance that his so many ingenious ways of showing that he recognized his commonness could present him as secretly rare. (*Awkward Age*, p. 65)

Whimsical, intelligent, perceptive, Mitchy possesses the highly developed sensibility Van lacks; he truly appreciates Nanda's gift; he accepts her as she is, yet he fails to capture her imagination as a suitor. While this anomaly adds psychological verisimilitude to James's characterization of Nanda, it also raises the question of the novelist's attitude toward his heroine as projected through his portrait of her. In spite of the girl's vision of herself as the prototype of the exposed, "new" young woman, part of her is ashamed of and condemns the very species of which she is so positive an example. Nanda reflects the vestiges of James's own ambivalence toward his creation —the "aware" *jeune fille*. Just before Nanda tells Mr. Longdon she has decided to come and live with him at Beccles as his adopted daughter, the old gentleman expresses his sorrow at the futility of her love for Van; he then gives voice to his anger at the young man's failure to appreciate Nanda. The girl defends Vanderbank: "It's I who am the horrible impossible and who have covered everything else with my own impossibility." (*Awkward Age*, p. 454)

Nanda's inability to respond to Mitchy stems from this

conflict she has about herself. She sees her own inse-
curity reflected in Mitchy's self-deprecation. Nanda cannot love Mitchy because he is too much like that part of
herself which she has difficulty accepting. Like the girl,
Mitchy is sensitive and insecure; unlike her, he is weak
and this aspect of his character frightens Nanda. Her
identification with Mitchy is too strong to risk the possibility of discovering that she shares his weakness. She
demonstrates the extent of her identification when she
urges him to marry Aggie in order to "save" her from the
depravity of Buckingham Crescent. If she had not been
able to save herself, she can at least assure Mitchy's constant proximity to an innocence that can never be hers.
The young man half understands this:

"You say you want me to save her. But what you really mean,"
Mitchy resumed from the sofa, "isn't at all exactly that."
   Nanda, without heeding the remark, took in the sunshine.
"It will be charming now in the garden." . . .
   "Your hope is that—as I'm good enough to be worth it—
she'll save *me*."
   Nanda looked at him now. "She will, Mitchy—she *will!*"
(*Awkward Age*, p. 303)

As was the case with James in relation to the sheltered
jeune fille, part of Nanda sees Aggie's innocence for what
it is, scant preparation for the realities of mature living,
but another part of her envies Aggie's sheltered, serene
existence, the care with which she was nurtured. Early in
the novel she says to Van:

"And then there's Aggie," the girl pursued, "I mean for the
real old thing. . . . she's a miracle. If one could be her exactly,
absolutely, without the least little mite of change, one would
probably do the best thing to close with it. Otherwise—except
for anything *but* that—I'd rather brazen it out as myself."
(*Awkward Age*, p. 287)

After Mitchy marries Aggie, she promptly becomes involved in an affair with Lord Petherton. When Mitchy
confronts Nanda with Aggie's promiscuity, her response
is paradoxical, combining mature insight with a curious
lack of conscience at having forced her friend into what
will certainly prove an unfortunate marriage:

   "Aggie's only trying to find out—"
   "Yes—what?" he asked waiting.
   "Why what sort of a person she is. How can she ever have

known? It was carefully, elaborately hidden from her—kept so obscure that she could make out nothing. She isn't now like *me*."

He wonderingly attended. "Like you?"

"Why, I get the benefit of the fact that there was never a time when I didn't know *something* or other and that I became more and more aware, as I grew older, of a hundred little chinks of daylight."

Mitchy stared. "You're stupendous, my dear!" he murmured.

Ah, but she kept it up. "*I* had my idea about Aggie."

"Oh, don't I know you had? And how you were positive about the sort of person—"

"That she didn't even suspect herself," Nanda broke in, "to be? I'm equally positive now. It's quite what I believed, only there's ever so much more of it. More *has* come—and more will yet. You see, when there has been nothing before, it all has to come with a rush. So that if even I am surprised, of course *she* is." (*Awkward Age*, p. 444)

If Nanda anticipated Aggie's irresponsible behavior after marriage, why then did she suggest that the sheltered *jeune fille* would save Mitchy? A possible explanation lies in Nanda's (and James's) ambivalent attitude toward exposure and the resulting awareness. Nanda does not "see" Aggie clearly until the end of the novel, after her own education has been completed; her earlier lack of perception in relation to Aggie stems from her feeling that the young girl is the embodiment of her own lost innocence. James either sensed the importance of incorporating this human frailty in his portrait of Nanda or, as artists so often do, unconsciously projected his own feelings through his art. Whatever motivated James to include this conflict in his characterization of Nanda, the result is a truthful rendering of human nature. A faithful representation of the complexities of the inner self necessitates a heroine divided within herself. The human situation does not allow for complete self-awareness. While Nanda comes closest to James's ideal—the perfect synthesis of intellect and emotion—she, like her creator, is human and therefore fallible. The contradiction in Nanda's feeling about what she is and what she would have liked to be makes it possible for her to describe herself to Mr. Longdon as "horrible" and "impossible" and then, almost in the same breath, to justify herself:

"We're many of us, we're most of us . . . extraordinary now. We can't help it. It isn't really our fault. There is so much else that's extraordinary that if we're in it all so much *we* must naturally be." (*Awkward Age*, pp. 456–57)

This inner contradiction makes her reject Mitchy and push him into a marriage with Aggie. In seeming to share Van's snobbery Nanda is really negating part of herself. In seeming to seek Mitchy's salvation, she is really seeking her own. Nanda eventually finds her salvation in an unqualified acceptance of self; but it did not come easily to her, just as James's solution to the problem of the European versus the American "way" did not come easily to him. Nanda possesses complete maturity when she finally accepts herself: "It was all obviously clearer to her than it had ever been, and her sense of it found renewed expression; so that she might have been, as she wound up, a very much older person than her friend." (*Awkward Age*, p. 457)

Little Aggie, imprisoned in her unawareness, victim of an education that offered empty convention instead of enlightened guidance is destined to perpetuate the hollow, inconsequential, and morally deficient life of the Brookenham set. In his final interview with Nanda, Mitchy observes:

Aggie is . . . already, and is likely to be still more, in what is universally recognized as your mother's regular line. . . . The generations will come and go and the *personnel*, as the newspapers say, of the saloon will shift and change, but the institution itself, as resting on a deep human need, has a long course yet to run and a good work yet to do. *We* shan't last, but your mother will, and as Aggies is happily very young she's therefore provided for, in the time to come, on a scale sufficiently considerable to leave us just now at peace. (*Awkward Age*, p. 439)

Mitchy's cynicism, like Vanderbank's fear, keeps him tethered to the world of the Brookenhams. Nanda, however, expresses James's conviction that vision, will, and strength of character can change things, that it is the responsibility of the percipient to be guide and mentor to the less perceptive. Mitchy's insight, Nanda implies, is worthless if he does not act upon it:

"The great thing [says Nanda] is to be helpful."

"And in what way—?" Mitchy asked with his wonderful air of inviting competitive suggestions.

"Toward Aggie's finding herself. . . . It's you yourself, naturally," his companion threw off, "who can help most." (*Awkward Age*, p. 445)

Unfortunately for Aggie, Mitchy has neither the will nor the strength of character to help her find her better self. As Van did before him, he places the responsibility on Nanda's shoulders:

"Certainly, and I'm doing my best too [to help Aggie]. So that with such good assistance"—he seemed at last to have taken it all from her—"what is it, I again ask, that, as you request, I'm to leave to you?"

Nanda required, while he still waited, some time to reply. "To keep my promise."

"Your promise?"

"Not to abandon you."

"Ah," cried Mitchy, "that's better!"

"Then good-by!" she said.

"Good-by." But he came a few steps forward. "I *mayn't* kiss your hand?"

"Never."

"Never?"

"Never."

"Oh!" he oddly sounded as he quickly went out. (*Awkward Age*, pp. 445–46)

Thus Nanda makes crystal clear to Mitchy on what basis their future relations will rest. If she will not completely turn her back on the world of her mother's saloon, it will be for the sole purpose of having a hand in the *real* education of Aggie, a sound, realistic, and redemptive course of instruction that does not include a flirtation with that young woman's husband; there is a suggestion that Buckingham Crescent may yet find a formidable opponent in Beccles.

Implicit in Nanda's frustrated love for Vanderbank is a condemnation of the society of which he is a part. Nanda's judgment on the values of Van's world is fully understood by him, but her repudiation of them poses a challenge the young man is unable to meet. Van "sees" but is slothful because his vision of Nanda's vision is too threatening for him. Where Van is afraid, Mitchy is indifferent; both lack the responsibility essential to maturity. In Nanda's renunciation of both Buckingham Crescent and the possibility of a fulfilled, normal life as wife and mother lies her public disavowal of an hypocritical and immoral society in which normal relationships cannot be sustained. The private act is transformed into one of universal significance. James is saying that true morality lies in the deepest possible perception of life; a world that does not recognize this is a world in moral chaos. The educative process requires the broadest exposure, but awareness without discrimination, knowledge without responsibility, insight without the will and strength to act is of scant value. Those accountable to the child must be selflessly involved in her life, feel genuine affection for her, and set an example worthy of emulation. A highly developed consciousness does not secure the child against suffering and defeat; only love and familial responsibility can mitigate the inevitable pain of living. These, then, are the laws that, in James's world, govern emotional and intellectual growth. They are the final and irrevokable answers to questions tentatively raised in the author's first novel of adolescence, at the outset of his career.

One need only compare the denouement of his earliest work on this theme with that of his last in order to take the measure of James's artistic development in the intervening years. Situation, character, even dialogue in the final scenes of *Watch and Ward* and *The Awkward Age* are strikingly similar yet undeniably different; thematic and technical changes reflect the essential difference between the young writer of 1871 and the mature artist of 1899. The basic situations are the same. In both cases the adolescent heroine, her education complete, is about to enter adulthood. Both young girls confront the men with whom they will spend the rest of their lives.

Nora Lambert, the heroine of the early work, has fled from her guardian, Roger Lawrence, because she is frightened by his proposal of marriage. She has learned, however, that the men she admired most (Fenton and Hubert) are not worthy of her affection, and that Roger, who has followed her in order to plead his cause, is the

only man of integrity in her life: "Nora read silently in
his haggard eyes the whole record of his suffering. It is a
strange truth that this seemed the most beautiful thing
she had ever looked upon; the sight of it was delicious. It
seemed to whisper louder and louder the secret about
Roger's heart. (*Watch and Ward*, p. 237) Nora's response
is sentimental in the extreme. Obvious suffering in a man
is more likely to repel the woman who has caused it than
attract her, and frustration in a relationship with one
man does not ignite the spark of love for another; it is
more apt to foster hate or at least resentment. The reader
is asked to accept the notion that Nora has suddenly
"seen the light" and will henceforth love and cherish her
former guardian in his new role of lover; she will presumably make the transition from daughter to wife with
no difficulty at all. The scene as presented is less than
convincing and the overwrought diction detracts from
the credibility of the character.

Nanda Brookenham, of *The Awkward Age*, finds herself
in a more believable situation. The person Nanda was, all
that happened to her during the course of the novel, led
inevitably to this moment in her life. Like Nora before
her, Nanda realizes that her future lies with her guardian, but there is a crucial difference. Since James has not
placed Nanda in the position of literally choosing to
marry her father, the emphasis can be shifted to a more
complex and interesting aspect of her relationship with
Mr. Longdon—the girl's moral commitment to her guardian and her need to retain her own identity. The sexual
overtones are muted; the erotic implication of the older
man's feeling for the young girl is relegated to a minor
position. Thus the scene in the later work has gained a
dimension totally missing in its counterpart in *Watch
and Ward*.

Both heroines are impelled to keep nothing back from
the men to whom they decide to entrust their lives. Nora
feels obligated to let Roger know that she has been ac-
cused of being "shameless" by Hubert's fiancée:

"Come," he said; "come!"
But she detained him, laying her other hand on his arm.

"No; you must understand first. If I am wiser now, I have learnt wisdom at my cost. I am not the girl you proposed to on Sunday. I feel—I feel *dishonored!*" she said, uttering the words with a vehemence that stirred his soul to its depths.

"My own poor child!" he murmured staring. (*Watch and Ward*, pp. 237–38)

Nothing in the text suggests that Nora has been "dishonored"; she has no real basis for feeling so. She has merely been subjected to an unpleasant scene with Hubert's fiancée. As presented, that young lady is abnormally suspicious and unbelievably aggressive. The reader takes a dim view of her ranting, as should Nora, if she were truly mature. Since obviously the young James meant us to take the fiancée seriously, Nora's gesture in repeating the jealous woman's absurd accusations is an empty one; the effort to convince Roger of her "dishonor" becomes trivial, and it follows that Roger's magnanimity becomes vacuous.

Nanda, on the other hand, because of the clearly defined and consistent character she is, poses a real dilemma for Mr. Longdon. She embodies a habit of mind alien to him, and the girl, who is aware of this, must be certain that the older man truly understands the nature of the young woman he has asked to share his life:

"Come!" he [Longdon] then very firmly said. . . .

She paused, but clearly for assent. "That's what I mean by your taking me as I am. It *is*, you know, for a girl—extraordinary."

"Oh, I know what it is!" he exclaimed with an odd weariness in his tenderness. (*Awkward Age*, pp. 456–57)

In making peace with Nanda's precocity, exposure, and sophistication, Longdon is doing more than accepting the young woman he cares for; he is embracing a new principle of growth, a new way of judging people and situations. The old man's "weariness" is understandable. Unlike Roger's "Come!", Longdon's summons implies a fresh approach to the educative process. In *The Awkward Age* James has placed the personal dilemma in a clearly defined social and philosophical context.

Both his men, of the early work and the late, in strikingly similar language, accept the "limitations" of the young women they love:

Roger gave a glance at the house behind them, as if to fling defiance and oblivion upon all that it suggested and contained. Then turning to Nora with a smile of exquisite tenderness: "My dear Nora, what have *we* to do with Hubert's young girls?" (*Watch and Ward*, p. 238)

And Mr. Longdon:

> "For some different person [says Nanda] you *could* have done what you speak of, and for some different person you can do it still."
> He stared at her with his barren sorrow. . . . "And what interest have I in any such person?" (*Awkward Age*, pp. 454–55)

Roger's "tender smile" and Longdon's "barren sorrow" seen thus in apposition become emblematic of the temporal, emotional, and intellectual gulf that separates the two works. The youthful Roger's acceptance of Nora (whom he has no reason to reject) is, like his "tender smile," superficial and ultimately inconsequential. The old man's acceptance of Nanda, on the other hand, is "barren" only in the sense that their relationship will never be consummated sexually; it is rich, however, in its suggestion of the complexity of human feelings. Longdon's concession is connotative because Nanda has come to represent a whole philosophy of life, one that he finally embraces after considerable inner conflict. If we accept the premise that James is speaking through Longdon (and it is not an unreasonable assumption) then it becomes an epistemology that the novelist has arrived at after years of observing the human scene and decades of experimenting with his art form.

James created his most important fictional children within a period of eight years (1891–99). This suggests that in the last decade of the nineteenth century he was impelled to reach back to his earlier self in his fiction in order to redefine attitudes, feelings, and concepts about growth and maturation which had lain dormant during years of preoccupation with other themes. He felt the need, it would appear, to return to his earliest phase as a novelist to re-examine old motifs in the light of his accumulated experience. Nanda Brookenham is the appropriate culmination of James's effort, during this retrospective period, to trace the development of the child through adolescence to maturity. Nora, Pansy, the governess, the telegraphist, and ultimately Nanda reflect the evolution of an artist in pursuit of a faithful representation of the inner life of the adolescent. These young people speak, as well, of the author's abiding concern with internal and external conditions that determine the emotional, intellectual, and moral complexion of the emerging adult.

CHAPTER X

The Jamesian Child
Conclusions

Any final statement about Henry James's contribution to child portraiture in fiction must speak of his weakness as well as his strength. A unique Jamesian child emerges from this study, one with identifiable characteristics that mark him as the novelist's very own, reflecting his creator's peculiar habit of mind and feeling. Any projection so intensely personal will not always correspond to our own experience with children or observations of childhood. Compared with children in the real world—and even with other novelist's representation of them—James's young people are, without doubt, too knowledgeable for comfort, too perceptive for ready acceptance. Increasingly the novelist subordinated other values to that of intellectual perspicacity; feeling became subsumed in cognition, ordinary human behavior in the exceptional posture, until his children and adolescents finally appeared as either incapable of sustaining all their knowledge or as over-prepared for what life could conceivably bring them. Their "seeing" and "knowing" became an end in itself, not quite justified by the moral superiority James ascribes to such vision. His important children possess excessive curiosity and this makes the reader uneasy in their presence and wary of identifying with them. The fact that so many of them are memorable in spite of this is a tribute to James's sincerity and dedication and to his consummate skill as a writer.

In 1865 James said that "a man's childhood and his manhood can never, without violation of truth, be made the same story. . . ."[1] In spite of his oft-stated conviction on this matter of blending man and child in fiction, he was himself guilty of erasing the distinction between them. In the final analysis, his children are, without exception, deeply sentient miniature adults. In his representation of youth he has avoided the sentimental and the puerile, but his young people are a shade too watchful and precious. The Jamesian child has all the attributes of the distinctive Jamesian heroine—and this is true of his little boys as well as his little girls; adult and child, therefore, tend to become one undifferentiated being. We must remember, however, that both child and adult in James's fiction are constructs of an imagination that sought primarily to create art out of reality; the novelist's aim was to illuminate fundamental possibilities of attitude and approach to life rather than faithfully to mirror it. He was artist enough not to seek a one-to-one correspondence with characters and events in the real world but instead to shed light on, and often criticize, existing climates of feeling or behavior through fictional representation. Because of his primary purpose, his young people often lack verisimilitude. In his rendering of younger children, theme invariably takes precedence over characterization. Dolcino, Morgan, Maisie, Flora, and Miles are all, with varying degrees of involvement and intensity, tactically engaged in giving formal expression to their creator's philosophy of childhood. In the main, James treated his young children symbolically; this enabled him to endow them with extraordinary perception and sensitivity. Eustace's response to his mother's marriage, Hyacinth's reaction to Holloway Gaol, and Maisie's moment of revelation about her true function in the lives of her parents are memorable examples of an uncanny grasp of what the child's world is really like.

James's adolescents are "done" with even greater psychological truth than are his younger children. This would seem to be logical, since they are closer to the adult habit of mind with which the novelist was more

1. Henry James, *Notes and Reviews* (Cambridge, Mass., 1921), p. 96.

familiar, and, by the time he created them, he had already been through the exercise of developing his younger children. With the notable exception of Nora Lambert of *Watch and Ward* and Effie of *The Other House,* young children precede adolescents and adolescents precede his richest and most complex phase as a novelist. We note with interest, however, that these adolescents are all young girls. Little boys do not survive to adolescence and this fact, as well as his continuing admiration for the strong *mère de famille,* raises many questions about the author's attitude toward the relative strength of men and women. Such questions lead inevitably to biography. But, if we set biography aside as not relevant to this study, these female adolescents suggest that the artistic temperament found fuller and freer expression through the personae of the strong, triumphant young woman. Viewed in this way, his girl-child becomes emblematic of intellectual, emotional, and spiritual development; all little girls blend to become one little girl who, like her creator, becomes more mature from tale to tale, conscientiously forging for herself (and possibly for James) a unique defense against the pain of a basically disillusioned view of life. This defensive mechanism—a fully and completely developed sensibility—assures survival and, because of its moral coloration, transcendence for child and author; in its artistic manifestation this transcendence becomes immortality through the creative act. Since James's voice is always clearly heard through the divining intelligence of his central characters, we are led to conclude that James's adolescents more nearly approximate real people because they more clearly project the personality of their author. Nanda Brookenham is the most convincing of the novelist's emerging adults perhaps because she expresses the compromise with the life of the senses which James must have reached at the end of the nineteenth century; she is emblematic, as well, of his resolution of the problem so central to James's thought and feeling—the European as opposed to the American way of preparing the young for adulthood.

Henry James's contribution to child portraiture in

fiction is considerable, but it is to be found in the assumptions that lie behind his rendering of the young rather than in his actual presentation of them. It is to be found in his nonfictional statements of principle as well as in his fictionalized philosophical comments on the relation between child and adult and the education of the young. In both instances his views are forward-looking and reflect attitudes that we have come to associate with the twentieth-century mind. James was a sensitive register and supporter of the revolution taking place during the nineteenth century which was to affect profoundly rapport between the generations. In 1895, James Sully, the British psychologist, pointed out that "the child not only observes but begins to reflect on what he observes, and does his best to understand the puzzling scene which meets his eye."[2] He might well have been describing the best of James's portraits of children. The intuition of the creative artist had led him to discover truths that psychologists were later to corroborate in their investigations of behavior in the young. Children are indeed aware and responsive to their environment, and to present them in literature as emotionally and intellectually in quarantine was, for James, evidence of failure of perception and a negation of the novelist's art. Children in life and in art had to be reckoned with; this fact became increasingly clear as the century progressed and James's writing supports this contention. On the other hand, he was critical of over-permissiveness at a time when the change in the intellectual climate was beginning to produce drastic rejection of the traditional Victorian concept of child-rearing. He foresaw that the pendulum would, of necessity, swing in the other direction, that parental dereliction could very easily take the form of parental license. James maintained a balanced view of the role of the child in society and in fiction; in both instances, however, children could no longer be assumed to be immune to experience.

Twentieth-century novelists owe a debt of gratitude to

2. James Sully, *Studies of Childhood* (New York, 1895), p. 65.

Henry James for his active role in the movement to sweep away outmoded convention and prejudice and to establish the child in literature as a worthy object of complete and honest investigation. In his preface to *What Maisie Knew*, the author articulated what he had long demonstrated in his fiction:

> Nothing of course . . . is an older story to the observer of manners and the painter of life than the grotesque finality with which such terms as "painful," "unpleasant," and "disgusting" are often applied to his results; . . . of course under that superstition I was punctually to have had read to me the lesson that the "mixing-up" of a child with anything unpleasant confessed itself an aggravation of the unpleasantness, and that nothing could well be more disgusting than to attribute to Maisie so intimate an "acquaintance" with the gross immoralities surrounding her. . . . The painter of life has indeed work cut out for him when a considerable part of life offers itself in the guise of that sapience.[3]

Evil exists in the world of the child as well as in that of the adult and for the novelist to pretend otherwise was, for James, unthinkable. He believed, and dramatized in his fiction, the notion that some primary form of understanding, a feeling for truth planted in us in infancy, is at the root of the moral sense. Maisie's exposure to evil, and her ability, in the face of such exposure, to transcend it, attests the strength of this primary knowledge basic to the human species. James was not alone in his conviction that the moral sense had its inception in infancy:

> I believe the growth of a moral sentiment, of that feeling of reverence for duty to which Kant gave such eloquent an expression, can only be understood by the most painstaking observation of the mental activities of the first years. May it, then, not well be that when a preternatural pressure of circumstance pushes the child over the boundary line of truth, he feels a shock, a horror, a giddy and aching sense of having violated law—law not wholly imposed by the mother's command, but rooted in the very habits of social life?[4]

By emphasizing the primacy of personal experience and intuitive response, Dr. Sully takes what is almost an

---

3. Henry James, *The Art of the Novel*, ed. R. P. Blackmur (New York, 1934), pp. 148–49.
4. Sully, *Studies of Childhood*, p. 265.

existential position, as does James in his insistence on the importance of felt life. Cognition looms too large in James's philosophy to label it existential, yet we detect strains of this important twentieth-century school of thought in his subject if not in his method of presentation. James's novels and tales are carefully structured in the Aristotelian tradition, but thematically he is dealing with ambiguity in a brutal and irrational world. And he is insisting, in his fictional as well as his nonfictional product, that the novelist's eye be penetrating and true. *All* of life, he had said, was the province of the creative artist; James's effort to place evil in the eye of the beholder was instrumental in stripping the veil of hypocrisy from contemporary representations of children, and, by extension, from all fictional portraiture.

James gave the child a psychic identity he had rarely had before. Dickens' children had been "vessels of grace"; with James, they become "vessels of consciousness." With his emphasis on the importance of the child's perceptive faculty, he anticipated method and theme of many twentieth-century novelists. In his compassion for the victimized child, James is solidly in the tradition of his romantic predecessors, but with his sensitive exploration of the child's consciousness and with his shift in emphasis from the physical to the psychological exploitation of the young, he moved directly into the main current of the twentieth-century inward-looking novel. During the 1890's, when James's child became more specifically a voluble commentator on the vagaries of a corrupt society, the novelist conceived of a function for his "convenient little image" which was to serve faithfully future critics of the social scene. James raised questions in his epistemological and metaphysical novels which prefigure the fundamental concern of twentieth-century man. The problem of how man can, within the world of his individual capacity, achieve a wholeness of self and learn to live with the duality and ambivalence of experience, was crucial for James. This question has become increasingly relevant for artists—indeed for all men—destined to live in a fragmented age of confusion and anxiety.

In his development of the theme of the sacrificial child as an instrument of adult aggression and hostility, James touched a deeply responsive chord in his reader and suggested a fruitful area of exploration for writers who followed him. As society continues to face the disintegration of an identifiable social and moral order, as the chasm between what is said and what is practiced becomes ever wider, the need for a scapegoat becomes increasingly urgent. The child, particularly in interpersonal relationships, is too often sacrificed on the altar of adult frustration. The twentieth-century novelist has found James's theme of the sacrificial child not only relevant to our troubled time but a reflection of it. James's emphasis on the moral separation of the child from the iniquitous world of the adult sounds the note of isolation that defines twentieth-century man. In his preface to "The Altar of the Dead," the novelist characterizes his world as being "under the awful doom of dehumanization." The projection of the child as an isolated individual gives dramatic substance to the theme of alienation which permeates modern fiction and adumbrates the dark view of childhood which we have come to associate with this era.

Henry James's modernity has been remarked upon by many critics of his work and it is palpably there for the reader to extract from his fiction. The fact that this modernity emerges as characteristic of his vision of childhood and adolescence comes as no surprise; one is struck rather by the depth of his perception of young people and the extent of his commitment to them. To those who charge James with creating characters that live almost entirely "off the top of their minds," [5] one can only suggest that even such early tales as "Master Eustace" and early novels such as *Washington Square* are vigorous refutations of the notion. Eustace, Catherine, Hyacinth, Morgan, Maisie, the governess and Nanda, to mention but a few of his young people, demonstrate that James had more than a surface understanding of un-

5. F. O. Matthiessen, *The James Family* (New York, 1947), p. 355.

conscious processes and that he drew upon this understanding in his rendering of children and adolescents in his novels and tales.

The exposed, aware, often sacrificed, more often transcendent Jamesian child touches us not because of his correspondence to actuality but because he speaks of another kind of reality—the reality of the felt, the inner life—that is not bound by temporal or geographic considerations. These young people, in spite of their excessive precocity, or maybe even because of it, prod us into an awareness of a more significant truth than can be projected through the faithful representation of externals; they force us to face the deeper truth of our precarious existence in a confusing and increasingly hostile environment. Through his fictional representation of childhood and adolescence, James strengthens our conviction that his was a total vision of the human condition. By dramatizing the plight of the victimized child and adolescent, Henry James was urging us to take the measure of ourselves and the world we were creating. If novelists have done this before, they have only rarely accomplished it with comparable sensitivity and power.

Bibliography

WORKS BY HENRY JAMES: FICTION AND NON-FICTION

The following tales and novels were selected for the purpose of this study:

"A Tragedy of Error"	1864	*The Princess Casamas-*	
"My Friend Bingham"	1867	*sima*	1886
"Osborne's Revenge"	1868	"A London Life"	1888
"A Problem"	1868	"The Patagonia"	1888
"Gabrielle De Bergerac"	1869	"The Pupil"	1891
"Daisy Miller"	1878	"Greville Fane"	1892
Watch and Ward	1878	*The Other House*	1896
Washington Square	1881	*What Maisie Knew*	1897
The Portrait of a Lady	1881	"The Turn of the Screw"	1898
"The Point of View"	1882	"In the Cage"	1898
"Pandora"	1884	*The Awkward Age*	1899
"The Author of		*The Ambassadors*	1903
Beltraffio"	1884	*The Golden Bowl*	1904
The Bostonians	1886		

Non-Fiction

The American Essays of Henry James, ed. Leon Edel. New York, 1956.

The American Scene, ed. W. H. Auden. New York, 1946.

The Art of the Novel, ed. R. P. Blackmur. New York, 1934.

English Hours. New York, 1905.

The Letters of Henry James, ed. Percy Lubbock. 2 vols. New York, 1920.

Literary Reviews and Essays, ed. Albert Mordell. New York, 1957.

The Middle Years. London, 1917.

"The New Year in England," *The Nation,* XXVIII (January 23, 1879), 65.

Notes and Reviews. Cambridge, Mass., 1921.

The Notebooks of Henry James, ed. F. O. Matthiessen and Kenneth B. Murdock. New York, 1962.

Notes of a Son and Brother. New York, 1914.

Notes on Novelists. New York, 1916.

Partial Portraits. London, 1919.

Portraits of Places. Boston, 1885.

The Selected Letters of Henry James, ed. Leon Edel. New York, 1955.

A Small Boy and Others. New York, 1913.

WORKS ON HENRY JAMES

Anderson, Quentin. *The American Henry James*. New Brunswick, N.J., 1957.
Andreas, Osborn. *Henry James and the Expanding Horizon*. Seattle, 1948.
Beach, James Warren. *The Method of Henry James*. New York, 1918.
Bewley, Marius. *The Complex Fate*. London, 1952.
Bowden, Edwin J. *The Themes of Henry James*. New Haven, 1956.
Cargill, Oscar. *The Novels of Henry James*. New York, 1961.
Clair, John A. *The Ironic Dimension in the Fiction of Henry James*. Pittsburgh, 1965.
Cranfil, Thomas Mabry and Robert Lanier Clark, Jr. *An Anatomy of "The Turn of the Screw."* Austin, 1965.
Dupee, F. W. *Henry James*. New York, 1956.
Edel, Leon. *Henry James*, Vol. I, *The Untried Years: 1843–1870*. New York, 1953.
————. *Henry James*, Vol. II, *The Conquest of London: 1870–1881*. New York, 1962.
————. *Henry James*, Vol. III, *The Middle Years: 1882–1895*. New York, 1962.
Edgar, Pelham. *Henry James, Man and Author*. Toronto, 1927.
Ford Madox Ford. *Henry James: A Critical Study*. New York, 1915.
Gale, Robert L. *The Caught Image: Figurative Language in the Fiction of Henry James*. Chapel Hill, 1964.
Hoffmann, Charles G. *The Short Novels of Henry James*. New York, 1957.
Holland, Laurence B. *The Expense of Vision: Essays on the Craft of Henry James*. Princeton, 1964.
Jefferson, D. W. *Henry James*. New York, 1961.
————. *Henry James and the Modern Reader*. New York, 1964.
Kelley, Cornelia P. *The Early Development of Henry James*. New York, 1930.
Kimbrough, Robert, ed. *The Turn of the Screw: An Authoritative Text, Background and Sources, Essays in Criticism*. New York, 1966.
Krook, Dorothea. *The Ordeal of Consciousness in Henry James*. Cambridge, England, 1962.
Matthiessen, F. O. *Henry James: The Major Phase*. New York, 1944.
————. *The James Family*. New York, 1947.
McCarthy, Harold T. *Henry James: The Creative Process*. New York, 1958.
Nowell-Smith, Simon. *The Legend of the Master*. New York, 1948.
Putt, S. Gorley. *A Reader's Guide to Henry James*. Ithica, 1967.
Stafford, William T., ed. *Perspectives on James's "The Portrait of a Lady": A Collection of Critical Essays*. New York, 1967.

Stevenson, Elizabeth. *The Crooked Corridor: A Study of Henry James*. New York, 1949.
Stone, Edward. *The Battle and the Books: Some Aspects of Henry James*. Athens, Ohio, 1964.
Swan, Michael. *Henry James*. London, 1952.
Vaid, Krishna Baldev. *Techniques in the Tales of Henry James*. Cambridge, Mass., 1964.
Ward, J. A. *The Imagination of Disaster: Evil in the Fiction of Henry James*. Lincoln, Nebr., 1961.
———. *The Search for Form: Studies in the Structure of James's Fiction*. Chapel Hill, 1967.
Wiesenfarth, Joseph. *Henry James and the Dramatic Analogy*. New York, 1963.

STUDIES AND CRITICAL ESSAYS ON HENRY JAMES IN BOOKS AND PERIODICALS

Aldrich, C. Knight. "Another Twist to *The Turn of the Screw*," *Modern Fiction Studies*, XIII, No. 2 (Summer, 1967), 167–78.
Allott, Miriam. "Symbol and Image in the Later Work of Henry James," *Essays in Criticism*, III (July, 1953), 321–36.
Aswell, E. Duncan. "James's *In the Cage*: The Telegraphist as Artist," *Texas Studies in Literature and Language*, VIII, No. 3 (Fall, 1966), 375–84.
———. "Reflections of a Governess: Image and Distortion in 'The Turn of the Screw'"; *Nineteenth-Century Fiction*, Vol. 23 (June, 1968), 49–63.
Banta, Martha. "Henry James and 'The Others,'" *The New England Quarterly*, XXXVII (June, 1964), 171–84.
Bantock, G. H. "Morals and Civilization in Henry James," *Cambridge Journal*, VII (December, 1953), 159–81.
Bass, Eben. "Dramatic Scene and *The Awkward Age*," *PMLA*, LXXIX (March, 1964), 148–57.
———. "Lemon-colored Volumes and Henry James," *Studies in Short Fiction*, I (Winter, 1964), 113–22.
Bewley, Marius. "Maisie, Miles and Flora, The Jamesian Innocents," *Scrutiny*, 17 (Autumn, 1950), 255–63.
Brebner, Adele. "How to Know Maisie," *College English*, XVII (February, 1956), 283–85.
Cambon, Glauco. "What Maisie and Huck Knew," *Studi Americani*, VI (1960), 203–20.
Canby, Henry S. *Turn West: Turn East: Mark Twain and Henry James*. Boston, 1951.
Cargill, Oscar. "Henry James's 'Moral Policeman,' William Dean Howells," *American Literature*, XXIX (May, 1957), 371–98.
———. "*The Turn of the Screw* and Alice James," *PMLA*, LXXVIII (June, 1963), 238–49.
Cooney, Séamus. "Awkward Ages in *The Awkward Age*," *Modern Language Notes*, LXXV (March, 1960), 208–11.
Dauner, Louise. "Henry James and the Garden of Death," *University of Kansas City Review*, XIX (Winter, 1952), 137–43.
Domaniecki, Hildegard. "Die Daumen Schrauben Der Erzie-

hung: Eine Interpretation Der Short Story 'The Turn of the Screw,'" *Text Und Kritik,* Vol. 15/16 (December, 1966), 44–61.

Edel, Leon. "Introduction," *The Ghostly Tales of Henry James.* New Brunswick, N.J., 1948.

――――. "The Literary Convictions of Henry James," *Modern Fiction Studies,* III (Spring, 1957), 3–10.

――――, ed. *Twentieth Century Views: Henry James.* Englewood Cliffs, N.J., 1963.

Emerson, Donald. "Henry James: A Sentimental Tourist and Restless Analyst," *Transactions of the Wisconsin Academy of Science, Arts and Letters,* LII (1963), 17–25.

Engelberg, E. "James and Arnold: Conscience and Consciousness in a Victorian Künstlerroman," *Criticism,* 10 (Spring, 1968), 93–114.

Farrea, Alison. "Watch, Ward, The Jamesian Themes," *Balcony: The Sydney Review,* 1 (1965), 23–27.

Firebaugh, Joseph. "The Pragmatism of Henry James," *Virginia Quarterly Review,* XXVII (Summer, 1951), 427–29.

Fish, Charles. "Form and Revision: The Example of *Watch and Ward,*" *Nineteenth-Century Fiction,* Vol. 22, No. 2 (September, 1967), 173–90.

Fraser, John. "*The Turn of the Screw* Again," *Midwest Quarterly,* VII, No. 4 (Summer, 1966), 327–36.

Füger, Wilhelm. "'In the Cage'—Versuche Zur Deutung Einer Umstrittenem Henry James Novelle," *Die Neueren Sprachen,* 15 (November, 1966), 506–13.

Gale, Robert L. "A Note on Henry James's First Short Story," *Modern Language Notes,* LXXII (January, 1957), 103–7.

――――. "Henry James's Dream Children," *Arizona Quarterly,* XV (Spring, 1959), 56–63.

――――. "Names in James." *Names,* Vol. 14, No. 2 (June, 1966), 83–108.

Gargano, James W. "What Maisie Knew: The Evolution of a 'Moral Sense,'" *Nineteenth-Century Fiction,* XVI (June, 1961), 34–46.

Goddard, Harold C. "A Pre-Freudian Reading of *The Turn of the Screw,*" *Nineteenth-Century Fiction,* XII (June, 1957), 1–36.

Habegger, Alfred C. "Secrecy in the Fiction of Henry James," *Dissertation Abstracts,* 28 (September–October, 1967), 1077A–78A.

Hall, W. F. "James's Conception of Society in *The Awkward Age,*" *Nineteenth-Century Fiction,* Vol. 23, No. 1 (June, 1968), 28–48.

Hamblen, A. A. "Henry James and the Power of Eros: What Maisie Knew," *Midwest Quarterly,* 9 (July, 1968), 391–99.

Haney, Charles William. "The Garden and the Child: A Study of Pastoral Transformation," *Dissertation Abstracts,* XXVI (1965), 2212.

Hartsock, Mildred. "The Exposed Mind: A View of *The Awkward Age,*" *Critical Quarterly,* Vol. 9, No. 1 (Spring, 1967), 49–59.

Heilman, Robert B. "The Freudian Reading of *The Turn of the Screw,*" *Modern Language Notes,* LXII (November, 1947), 433–45.

———. "The Lure of the Demonic," *Comparative Literature,* XIII (Fall, 1961), 346–57.

Hill, Hamlin L., Jr. "The Revolt of the Daughters: A Suggested Source for *The Awkward Age,*" *Notes and Queries,* CCVI (January–December, 1961), 347–49.

Hopkins, Viola. "Visual Art Devices and Parallels in the Fiction of Henry James," *PMLA,* LXXVI (December, 1961), 561–74.

Hound and Horn, Vol. 7, No. 3 (October–September, 1934).

Hynes, Joseph A. "The Middle Way of Miss Farange: A Study of James's *Maisie,*" *ELH,* XXXII (1965), 528–33.

Ives, C. B. "James's Ghosts in *The Turn of the Screw,*" *Nineteenth-Century Fiction,* XVII (September, 1963), 183–89.

Johnson, Courtney, Jr. "The Problem of Sex in the Writings of Henry James," *Dissertation Abstracts,* 28 (July–August, 1967), 679A.

Katan, A. "A Causerie on Henry James's 'The Turn of the Screw,' " in *The Psychoanalytic Study of the Child,* ed. R. S. Eissler and others. 20 vols. New York, 1962.

Kimmey, John L. "The Princess Casamassima and the Quality of Bewilderment," *Nineteenth-Century Fiction,* Vol. 22, No. 1 (June, 1967), 47–62.

Knights, Lionel Charles. *Explorations: Essays in Criticism.* London, 1946.

Knox, George. "Incubi and Succubi in *The Turn of the Screw,*" *Western Folklore,* XXII (April, 1963), 122–23.

Lang, Hans-Joachim. "The Turns in *The Turn of the Screw,*" *Jahrbuch Fur Amerikastudien,* IX (1964), 110–28.

Leavis, F. R. "James's *What Maisie Knew:* A Disagreement," *Scrutiny,* XVII (Summer, 1950), 115–27.

Levin, Gerald. "Why Does Vanderbank not Propose?" *University of Kansas City Review* (June, 1961), 314–18.

Levy, Edward R. "Henry James and the Pragmatic Assumption: The Conditions of Perception," *Dissertation Abstracts,* XXV, Nos. 1, 2, 1964, 1212.

Levy, Leo B. "*The Turn of the Screw* as Retaliation," *College English,* XVII (February, 1956), 286–88.

Masback, Frederick Joseph. "The Child Character in Hawthorne and James," *Dissertation Abstracts,* XXI (July–September, 1960), 338.

McCloskey, John C. "What Maisie Knows: A Study of Childhood and Adolescence," *American Literature* (January, 1965), 485–513.

McElderry, B. R., Jr. "Henry James's Revision of *Watch and Ward,*" *Modern Language Notes* (November, 1952), 457–61.

Modern Fiction Studies, XII, No. 1 (Spring, 1966).

Monteiro, George. " 'Girlhood on the American Plan'—A Contemporary Defence of *Daisy Miller,*" *Books at Brown,* XIX (May, 1963), 89–93.

Moore, Rayburn S. "The Full Light of Higher Criticism: Edel's

Biography and Other Recent Studies of Henry James,"
South Atlantic Quarterly, LXIII, 1964, 104–14.

Newton, J. M. "Isabel Archer's Disease and Henry James,"
The Cambridge Quarterly, Vol. 21, No. 1 (Winter, 1966–67),
3–22.

Ohmann, Carol. "Daisy Miller: A Study of Changing Intentions," *American Literature,* XXXVI (March, 1964), 1–11.

Owen, Elizabeth. " 'The Awkward Age' And the Contemporary
English Scene," *Victorian Studies,* XI (September, 1967),
63–82.

Reilly, Robert J. "Henry James and the Morality of Fiction,"
American Literature, Vol. 39, No. 1 (March, 1967), 1–30.

Reiman, Donald H. "The Inevitable Imitation: The Narrator
in "The Author of Beltraffio," *Texas Studies in Literature
and Language,* III (Winter, 1962), 503–9.

Rozenzweig, Saul. "The Ghost of Henry James: A Study in
Thematic Apperception," *Character and Personality,* XII
(December, 1943), 79–100.

Rubin, Louis D., Jr. "One More Turn of the Screw," *Modern
Fiction Studies,* IX (Winter, 1963–64), 314–28.

Salomon, Roger B. "Realism as Disinheritance: Twain,
Howells and James," *American Quarterly,* XVI (Winter,
1964), 531–44.

Schneider, Sister Lucy, C.S.J. "Osculation and Integration:
Isabel Archer in the One-Kiss Novel, *College Language Association Journal,* X, No. 2 (December, 1966), 149–61.

Scoggins, James. "The Author of Beltraffio: A Reapportionment of Guilt," *Texas Studies in Literature and Language,*
V (Summer, 1963), 265–70.

Sharp, Sister M. Corona. "Fatherhood in Henry James." *University of Toronto Quarterly,* XXXV, No. 3 (April, 1966),
279–92.

Short, R. W. "Henry James's World of Images," *PMLA,*
LXVIII (December, 1953), 943–60.

Snow, Lotus. "Some Small Stray Fragrance of an Ideal:
Henry James's Imagery for Youth's Discovery of Evil."
Harvard Library Bulletin, XIV (Winter, 1960), 107–25.

Solomon, Eric. "The Return of the Screw," *The University
Review,* XXX (Spring, 1964), 205–11.

Spilka, Mark. "Turning the Freudian Screw: How Not To Do
It," *Literature and Psychology,* XIII (Fall, 1963), 105–11.

Stein, William Bysshe. " 'The Pupil': The Education of a
Prude," *Arizona Quarterly,* XV (Spring, 1959), 13–22.

Tanner, Tony. *The Reign of Wonder: Naivety and Reality in
American Literature.* Cambridge, England, 1965.

Thorberg, Raymond. "Terror Made Relevant: James's Ghost
Stories." *Dalhousie Review,* 47 (Summer, 1967), 185–91.

Volpe, Edmond. "James's Theory of Sex in Fiction," *Nineteenth-Century Fiction,* XIII (June, 1958), 36–47.

Walsh, William. *The Use of the Imagination.* New York, 1960.

Ward, J. A. "The Double Structure of 'Watch and Ward,' "
Texas Studies in Literature and Language, IV (Winter,
1963), 613–24.

Ward, J. A. "James's Idea of Structure," *PMLA*, LXXX (September, 1965), 417–26.

Wasiolek, Edward W. "Maisie: Pure or Corrupt?" *College English*, XXII (December, 1960), 167–72.

West, Muriel. "The Death of Miles in *The Turn of the Screw*," *PMLA*, LXXIX (June, 1964), 238–49.

Willen, Gerald. ed. *A Casebook of Henry James's "The Turn of the Screw."* New York, 1959.

Winner, V. H. "Artist and the Man in 'The Author of Beltraffio," *PMLA*, 83 (March, 1968), 102–8.

Wilson, Edmund. "Books," *The New Yorker* (May 27, 1944), 72–82.

Wilson, Harris W. "What *Did* Maisie Know?" *College English*, XVII (February, 1956), 279–82.

Wolf, H. R. "What Maisie Knew: The Rankian Hero," *American Imago*, XXIII (Fall, 1966), 227–34.

Worden, Ward S. "A Cut Version of *What Maisie Knew*," *American Literature*, XXIV (January, 1953), 493–504.

———. "Henry James's *What Maisie Knew*: A Comparison with Plans in *The Notebooks*," *PMLA*, LXVIII (June, 1953), 371–83.

BACKGROUND MATERIAL

Abrams, M. H. *The Mirror and the Lamp.* New York, 1953.

Allen, Walter. *The English Novel.* London, 1954.

Avery, Gillian. *Nineteenth Century Children.* London, 1965.

Babenroth, A. Charles. *English Childhood: Wordsworth's Treatment of Childhood in the Light of English Poetry Prior to Crabbe.* New York, 1922.

Barrie, J. M. *Peter Pan and Wendy.* New York, 1940.

Beach, Joseph Warren. *English Literature of the Nineteenth and Early Twentieth Centuries: 1798 to the First World War.* New York, 1950.

Bernbaum, Ernest. ed. *Anthology of Romanticism.* 3rd ed. New York, 1948.

———. *Guide Through the Romantic Movement.* rev. ed. New York, 1949.

Blake, George. *Barrie and the Kailyard School.* London, 1951.

Blake, William. *The Poetical Works of William Blake.* London, 1913.

———. *Seven Songs from "Songs of Innocence."* London, (19——).

Bowen, Elizabeth. "The Bend Back," *Cornhill*, CLXV (Summer, 1951), 221–27.

Brennan, Bernard P. *The Ethics of William James.* New York, 1961.

Brophy, Brigid. "A Masterpiece, and Dreadful," *The New York Times Book Review* (January 17, 1965), 1.

Buckley, Jerome. *The Victorian Temper.* Cambridge, Mass., 1951.

Burnett, Frances Hodgson. *Little Lord Fauntleroy.* New York, 1886.

Caldwell, Elsie Noble. *Last Witness for Robert Louis Stevenson.* Norman, Okla., 1960.

Carrington, C. E. *The Life of Rudyard Kipling.* New York, 1955.

Carroll, Lewis. *Alice's Adventures in Wonderland.* London, 1949.

Cecil, David. *Max: A Biography.* London, 1964.

Coveney, Peter. *Poor Monkey: The Child in Literature.* London, 1957.

Croft-Cooke, Rupert. *Rudyard Kipling.* London, 1948.

Daiches, David. *Stevenson and the Art of Fiction,* New York, 1951.

Darton, F. J. Harvey. *Children's Books in England.* Cambridge, Eng., 1932.

Darwin, Charles. "Biographical Sketch of an Infant," *Mind,* II (July, 1877), 285.

Dickens, Charles. *David Copperfield.* London, 1938.

———. *Great Expectations.* London, 1938.

———. *Nicholas Nickleby.* London, 1957.

———. *Oliver Twist.* London, 1938.

Edel, Leon. *The Psychological Novel, 1900–1950.* London, 1955.

Empson, William. "Alice in Wonderland: The Child as Swain," in *The Critical Performance,* ed. Stanley Edgar Hyman. New York, 1956.

Eustace, Jennie A. "Kit: An American Boy," *Yellow Book,* XIII (April, 1897), 239.

Fairlie, Henry. "American Kids?" *The New York Times Magazine* (November 14, 1965), 116.

Freud, Sigmund. *An Outline of Psychoanalysis,* trans. James Strachey. New York, 1949.

Golding, William. *Lord of the Flies.* New York, 1955.

Hall, G. Stanley. *Adolescence,* Vol. I. New York, 1925.

Harlow, Virginia. *Thomas Sergeant Perry: A Biography.* Durham, N.C., 1950.

Hazard, Paul. *Les Livres, Les Enfants et Les Hommes.* Paris, 1932.

Hogan, John H., Jr. "The Poor Labyrinth: The Theme of Social Injustice in Dickens's Great Expectations," *Nineteenth-Century Fiction,* IX (October, 1954), 169–78.

Hughes, Richard. *A High Wind in Jamaica.* New York, 1929.

Johnson, Edgar. *Charles Dickens: His Tragedy and Triumph.* 2 vols. New York, 1952.

Jones, Ernest. *The Life and Work of Sigmund Freud.* 2 vols. New York, 1953–55.

Kazin, Alfred. "A Procession of Children," *The American Scholar* (Spring, 1964), 173.

Kipling, Rudyard. *Stalky & Co.* London, 1954.

Laski, Marghanita. *Mrs. Ewing, Mrs. Molesworth and Mrs. Hodgson Burnett.* London, 1950.

Levin, Harry. "Wonderland Revisited," *Kenyon Review,* XXVII, No. 4 (Autumn, 1965), 591–616.

Lewis, R. W. B. *The American Adam: Innocence, Tragedy and Tradition in the Nineteenth Century.* Chicago, 1955.

Lindsay, Jack. *Charles Dickens*. London, 1950.

Lubbock, Percy. *The Craft of Fiction*. New York, 1921.

Mackail, Denis. *Barrie, the Story of J.M.B.* New York, 1941.

Marcus, Steven. *Dickens: From Pickwick to Dombey*. New York, 1965.

Matthiessen, F. O. *The American Renaissance*. New York, 1941.

Mix, Katherine Lyon. *A Study in Yellow: The "Yellow Book" and Its Contributors*. Lawrence, Kans., 1960.

Muir, P. H. *English Children's Books, 1600-1900*. London, 1954.

Nelson, Kenneth M. "A Religious Metaphor," *Reconstructionist*, XXXI (November 26, 1965), 7-16.

Overton, Grant M. *The Women Who Make Our Novels*. New York, 1922.

Preyer, George W. *Mental Development in the Child*. New York, 1895.

Roth, Henry. *Call it Sleep*. New York, 1964.

Rourke, Constance. *American Humor*. New York, 1931.

————. *The Roots of American Culture*. New York, 1942.

Salinger, J. D. *The Catcher in the Rye*. Boston, 1951.

Stevenson, Robert Louis. *Treasure Island*. London, 1948.

Sulley, James. *Studies of Childhood*. New York, 1895.

Tompkins, Joyce M. S. *The Art of Rudyard Kipling*. London, 1959.

Twain, Mark. *Huckleberry Finn*. Cambridge, Mass., 1958.

Wharton, Edith. *A Backward Glance*. New York, 1934.

Wicksteed, Joseph H. *Blake's Innocence and Experience*. New York, 1928.

Wilson, Edmund. *The Wound and the Bow*. Boston, 1941.

Wordsworth, William. *The Complete Poetical Works of Wordsworth*. Boston, 1932.

Wright, Austin, ed. *Victorian Literature: Modern Essays in Criticism*. New York, 1961.

Young, G. M. *Victorian England: Portrait of an Age*. London, 1936.

Index

Adolescence, theme of, vii–viii, 146; problems of, 82, 127; modern vision of, 177–78

Adolescent, vii–viii, 131, 132–33, 135–36, 140, 141, 143, 144–45, 146, 147, 149, 157, 170, 171–73. *See also* Boy, Girl, *Jeune fille*

Adult, inhumanity and cruelty of, 10, 27, 112, 114, 152; egotism of, 72, 76, 110, 117, 151

Alcott, Louisa M., 16, 25, 41–42

Ambiguity of human experience, 22, 43, 76, 77, 90, 121, 131, 132, 137, 139, 144, 176

American-European traditions, 81; polarity, 93, 95, 96, 173

Appearance and reality, 136–37, 139, 154

Aristotelian tragedy, 14; tradition, 176

Artist, 4, 16, 59, 141; development of, 142

Artistic creation, qualities associated with, 75

Atlantic Monthly, 28, 100, 127

Barrie, J. M., 12–13, 20

Bell, John Jay, 12

Blake, William, 4–6; quoted, 5

Boy, American, 42; doomed not to survive, 29, 76–77, 92–93, 107–8, 135, 150, 173

Burnett, Frances H., 15

Carroll, Lewis, 16, 17, 22

Century Magazine, 47, 99

Charles, Mrs. E. R., 24

Chesterton, G. K., quoted, 23

Child, evolution of in fiction, viii, 8, 18, 22, 26–27, 32, 35, 40, 72, 77, 83, 107, 138–39, 169–70,

171–78 *passim;* classic view of, 3, 4; romantic view of, 6, 12; American, 7–8, 10–12, 15–16, 33–34, 41–42, 47–48; as victim or "sacrificed," 8–9, 20, 29–30, 39–40, 43, 57–58, 63, 72, 75–82 *passim,* 93, 104, 110–11, 125, 137, 176–78; capacity for evil in, 8, 18, 20, 22; precocious, 8, 34, 41, 83, 88–89, 91, 128–29, 138, 168; disinherited and dispossessed, 9, 68, 71; exposed to knowledge of good and evil, 11, 22, 34, 54, 98, 102, 103, 131–32, 136, 139, 150, 155, 156, 175; sentimental view of, 15, 24–25; as alien and isolated, 20, 177; quest for identity, 22, 71, 122; as miniature adult, 24, 172; as contrivance for dramatic action, 29–30; as pictorial embellishment, 31–32; "spoiled," 33, 39–42, 57, 60–62; rearing of, 35, 42, 81, 95, 174; and freedom, 34, 43, 92, 94, 95, 97, 103, 107; reversal of roles with parents, 51, 101, 119–20, 122, 135, 158; and vision of reality, 54, 61, 145, 146, 154; as product of environment, 63–65, 71; and heredity, 63, 71; used by adult as instrument of aggression, 64, 72, 78, 111–12; sensibility of, 68, 82, 102, 107, 122–23, 127; metaphorical use of, 78, 80, 126; ideal, 81–82; 125; as "seer," 84–85, 135; European, 95; awareness of self, 98, 103, 129, 133–34, 144, 163; as central intelligence and conscious agent, 109–10;